T0056865

the joy of
cheesemaking

the joy of

cheesemaking

**THE ULTIMATE GUIDE TO UNDERSTANDING,
MAKING, AND EATING FINE CHEESE**

Jody Farnham

Skyhorse Publishing

Copyright © 2011, 2015 by Jody Farnham

All rights reserved. No part of this book may be reproduced in any manner without the express written consent of the publisher, except in the case of brief excerpts in critical reviews or articles. All inquiries should be addressed to Skyhorse Publishing, 307 West 36th Street, 11th Floor, New York, NY 10018.

Skyhorse Publishing books may be purchased in bulk at special discounts for sales promotion, corporate gifts, fund-raising, or educational purposes. Special editions can also be created to specifications. For details, contact the Special Sales Department, Skyhorse Publishing, 307 West 36th Street, 11th Floor, New York, NY 10018 or info@skyhorsepublishing.com.

Skyhorse® and Skyhorse Publishing® are registered trademarks of Skyhorse Publishing, Inc.®, a Delaware corporation.

Visit our website at www.skyhorsepublishing.com.

10 9 8 7 6 5 4 3 2 1

Library of Congress Cataloging-in-Publication Data is available on file.

Cover photo from iStock

Print ISBN: 978-1-63220-466-0
Ebook ISBN: 978-1-63450-124-8

Printed in China

To my mom
For teaching me the meaning of *joie de vivre*
and
To my three daughters for reminding me to live it
every day

—Jody Farnham

CONTENTS

Introduction

YOU LOVE IT OR YOU HATE IT (and I haven't met too many cheese haters). The students who have attended classes at the Institute over the years have shown us a diversity of professional backgrounds. They come from all walks of life seeking to learn the science and the art of cheesemaking. From career changers like brain surgeons and art historians, to chefs looking to add cheesemaking to their growing list of on-farm restaurant practices, they all want to learn to make cheese.

I'm a child of the sixties, born and raised here in Vermont in the mythic place known as suburbia. On any given evening there would be forty-eight kids on my block showing up to play kick-the-can. I had five siblings, and I knew cheese as Kraft American slices sandwiched between two pieces of Wonder Bread and grilled.

Milk was delivered to our house a few days a week. Eggs, too. But for me the silver galvanized box with the word MILK stamped on the lid, out by the back stoop, was a place to hide the back door key, or to be commandeered for use as a boost to the first rung on the ladder to the tree house. Milk at that time never struck me as essential to all life, or related in any sense to cheese. Little did I know, it would become central to my life's work and passion.

And with this same passion, I have filled *The Joy of Cheesemaking* with helpful information, ideas, tips, and the basic steps for making cheese, so that hobbyists, enthusiasts, and professional cheesemakers alike will be able to use the practical science here in these chapters to get started in cheesemaking.

LEFT: Cabot Clothbound Cheddar
CREDIT: *Olivia Farnham*

You only need to know how to make a few basic cheeses in order to get started. I've included seven here. A world of possibilities opens up as you master the "make process" and start to add your own finesse and skill to the cheesemaking. I want you to get a glimpse of the cheese industry as a whole, including the technical side of making cheese, the science and best practices, and the practical side of this profession—what life is like outside the cheese house.

I have profiled a number of small cheesemaking farms around the country. Everyone has a story about how they got started in cheese. (Be sure to record yours someplace so you can share with us and the world later on.) The families and farms in these profiles have achieved something wonderful: a sustainable lifestyle on the land and with their animals. See what's cooking in the farm kitchens and try out some of the recipes. Cooking with cheese is a sustainably savory way to add even more value to your day, and may inspire you to create a tasty new recipe of your own.

Enjoy the stories about those who have gone ahead and carved out the lifestyle they dreamed of and you may be dreaming of, too! The book also introduces you to a number of cheesemakers who have been creating quality cheese and building integrity within the industry for years. I call them the "rock stars" of cheese, "Rockin' the Wedge" by bringing great vitality and industry to the world of cheese; we would not be as far along in this ever evolving industry without their valuable contributions. You will also find a chapter in here on the wonders of tasting and pairing cheese and the how-tos of impressing your next dinner guests with a gorgeous cheese board and some fun practical information about the cheese you are serving. I like to call it *informed entertainment*, kind of a new take on the old cocktail-party scene.

In cheesemaking, creating cheese by hand and working toward the art of the possible, you will find people to collaborate with. There are those people who will know a bit more about a certain aspect of cheesemaking than you do, such as the breed of animals you're milking or the seasonality of the milk, so don't be afraid to ask, reach out, and build a team of cheese experts who will support and nurture your project.

But most important, have fun!

Jody Farnham
Vermont, 2010

Cheddar cheese with trier, used to test the interior of the cheese for flavor profile development and grading.

PHOTO CREDIT: *Olivia Farnham*

ALL CHEESE

$5.00

① Cheese Classification

CHEESE CLASSIFICATION is simply identifying the "family" to which a cheese belongs. There are five classifications for all cheeses. We know that all cheese starts with the same ingredient—milk, whether cow's, goat's, sheep's, or water buffalo's (and in some parts of the world horse's and camel's). The cheeses that come from this milk are the result of what you, the cheesemaker, do with the milk. The quality of the milk, starter culture, technology, and the craft and aging expertise of the cheesemaker will combine to bring about biodiversity in any cheese.

Cheese biodiversity means the variations you will find among cheeses, which are affected by all of the elements comprising the cheesemaking process, including the breed of animal, the diet of the herd, equipment used in the production of the cheese, and the skill of the craftsperson; and the multiple microorganisms that grow in and on the surface of cheese, imparting their character and unique flavor profiles throughout the cheesemaking process and during aging.

There are two categories into which all cheese characteristics fall: The first is the *organoleptic perspective*. This refers to the texture, flavor, aroma, and rind composition of a cheese—meaning the appearance and sensory properties of a cheese; what you taste, see, smell and feel, both in your hands and on the mouth. The second category for characterizing cheese is the *physicochemical perspective*. This refers to the moisture, fat content, and the pH of a cheese. When classifying cheese, you are using both the appearance of the cheese and how you interact with it. Some call this the art. . . . as well as, additional scientific data we know in general to be true . . . of cheese, and this *is* the science of cheese.

The following classification of cheese will help you identify the proper characteristics of cheese and give you a general idea of what style of cheese falls into which family. When you find yourself at the farmers' market on Saturday morning, in a cheese shop, or participating in a wine and cheese tasting, you will then recognize that a Vermont Cheddar is a hard cheese or a Reblochon from France is a washed-rind cheese that belongs to the soft-ripened family . . . Voilà!

So head to cheese class . . . ification!

CHEESE STYLING			
Family of Cheese	Notes	Flavor	Try me
Fresh Cheese	bright white, fluffy, loose, no rind	milky, mild, tart lemony, tangy	fresh Chèvre, feta; queso blanco, quark
Soft-ripened Cheese	bright white exterior, fuzzy or wrinkled rind, orangish surface	buttery, mushroomy floral, musty, barnyard	Saint-Marcellin, Bijou, Camembert, Les Freres
Semihard Cheese	pale white, tiny openings, firm, variations of gray exterior	floral, sweet butter, slightly salty, sweet	Tomme de Savoie, Monterey Jack, Gouda
Hard Cheese	firm, compacted body, light yellow/golden paste	butterscotch, pineapple, earthy, salty, sweet	Cheddar, Comté, Manchego, Parmigiano-Reggiano
Blue Cheese	dark green/blue veining, firm, creamy, crumbly paste	bacon, caramel, smoky nutty, salty, buttery	Magtag Blue, Fourme d'Ambert, Gorgonzola, Cashel Blue

Fresh Cheese (soft, brined, whey, and pasta filata cheese)

The fresh cheese classification is a fairly large one, because it covers a wide range of cheese types. These cheeses feature fresh, milky, tangy, and in some cases salty notes, as in feta cheese. This category of cheese is referred to as "fresh" because the cheese is not "aged out" but is consumed quickly after production. When you think of fresh cheese, descriptors such as light white in color, fluffy, creamy comes to mind.

In fact, those are some of the basic organoleptic (sensory) characteristics of fresh cheese. Examples are: fromage blanc, Chèvre, cottage cheese, feta, ricotta, and mozzarella. The physicochemical properties, (moisture, fat, pH) in fresh cheese contribute to a body or paste that may be crumbly like queso blanco,

ABOVE: Smooth mozzarella pairs beautifully with tomatoes.

stretchy or smooth like mozzarella, custard-like and similar to fromage blanc, or a bit drier paste like fresh goat Chèvre. The physicochemical properties are determined by the addition of lactic acid bacteria (starter culture) and the amount of moisture retained in the cheese. Fresh cheese can contain up to 83 percent moisture. The high moisture content gives this family of cheese a short shelf life, between thirty and forty-five days after manufacture.

ABOVE: Pepper Chèvre from Pure Luck Farm

Aside from pasta filata cheese (meaning stretched), like Bocconcini and nonmelting cheese like queso blanco in this classification, these fresh lactic cheeses generally have a creamy constancy, are easy to make at home, and are worth the twenty-four-hour draining time necessary before you can enjoy the fruits—or in this case the cheeses—of your labor.

Soft-Ripened cheese (bloomy-rind and washed-rind)

Soft-ripened cheeses are just as their category name implies. For the most part, they are soft, runny, gooey mounds of unctuous goodness. They are generally aged for only a few weeks at a temperature between 10–15°C/50–59°F. Think Époisses from France, Redhawk from California, or a ripe Brie at room temperature perfection; all of these cheeses are considered to be soft-ripened.

Soft-ripened cheese is a large classification that has three categories of rind appearance. First, for the bloomy-rind cheeses there are two subcategories of rind development. The first is a wrinkled-looking cheese with a light bloom and intricate patterns of yeast and mold and a firmer body. The second has almost no appearance of wrinkles; it looks and feels smooth with a thin translucent rind of white fuzz. Both styles are considered bloomy-rind cheeses. The presence of *Geotrichum candidum* is predominant in all styles of cheese in the soft-ripened category. It has multiple purposes in the cheesemaking process (it can be added during the make or introduced in the aging room to varying degrees). *G. candidum* is the key to flavor development, aging, and rind composition for this family of cheese. Generally this type of soft, surface-ripened cheese is made from goat's milk and has a brittle texture but breaks down to a smooth, creamy goodness in the mouth.

LEFT: Surface-ripened cheese from Vermont Butter and Cheese Creamery. Cheese reference clockwise is: Bijou, Bonne Bouche, Coupole.
PHOTO CREDIT: *Lou Polish*

RIGHT: This bloomy-rind cheese is a gorgeous Camembert with a smooth, bright white surface, thanks to the presence of *Geotrichum candidum*, the key to flavor development, aging, and rind composition for this family of cheese.

The classification of soft-ripened cheese also includes a third category, washed-rind cheese. This is cheese with a sticky orange or reddish rind. Washed-rind cheese is a meaty, yeasty, barnyard-smelling cheese not for the faint of heart, but once you are past the sticky, grainy exterior you will find heaven. Washed-rind cheese has a sweet, savory smoothness that will melt in the mouth, generally less pronounced than the on-the-nose aroma, long on taste, and clean on the finish . . . Surprised? Try Oma, a newcomer from Vermont, or the classic Taleggio from Italy.

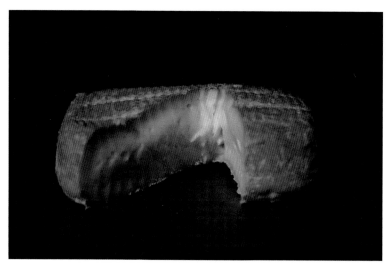

ABOVE: Washed-rind cheese has a very strong smell, but the cheese itself is long on taste and clean on the finish.

ABOVE: Carmonday, Bellwether Farm, Sonoma County, California.

Semi-hard cheese (pressed non-cooked)

The semi-hard cheese classification has more to do with the luscious texture of these cheeses and the fine pinhole openings or mechanical eyes you will see in the body of many of the cheeses in this class, rather than their understated, milder, more subtle flavors. Low moisture content, 50–55 percent, is helped along when the cheesemaker cuts the curds smaller than those of a soft-ripened cheese (see chapter 3). The knitting process (curds creating a community) (see chapter 5) is slowed down during the drain time and therefore not all the curds knit together tightly, leaving very tiny pinhole openings or eyes in the paste or body of the cheese.

Next the curds are molded and lightly pressed or weighted, by stacking the cheeses on top of each other. Once they can hold their shape they are salted and washed with a smearing solution

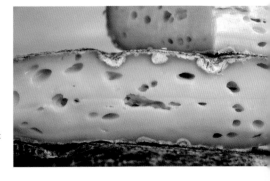

RIGHT: The knitting process (curds creating a community) is slowed down during the drain time, so curds do not knit tightly, leaving tiny openings or eyes in body of the cheese.

to encourage initial rind development. Sometimes the cheese is left
unwashed to create a natural rind.
After the cheese is placed in the
aging room or cave, washing may
continue depending on the style of
cheese being produced. A few classic
examples of cheese in this family are
Tomme de Savoie and St. Paulin from
France and the Gouda-style cheese
from Tumalo Farm, Oregon.

Some semi-hard cheeses in this
category do not have the characteristic tiny holes, but the texture will
be smooth, firm, and flexible, and the interior of the cheese will have a
creamy off-white or ivory color. Semi-hard cheeses are generally aged
sixty to seventy-five days. If you can control the moisture content in this
style of cheese you will have great success. This family of cheese is best
enjoyed with the culinary collaboration of cheese, bread, and heat! Can
you say fondue?

ABOVE: Get to know your cheese families. There are five classes of cheese in this
book; basic differences define each family. Read through and become familiar with the
similarities and differences between these families. Some cheese characteristics will be
the same from family to family classification, and many cheeses cross over and hang out
with more than one family at a time.

Hard cheese (extra-hard)

The hard cheese classification has a couple of branches on the family tree. The first category is hard cheese, like the Swiss-style Emmental or the classic from the Jura region of France, Comté. The hard cheese classification is just as it sounds; generally the cheese in this family is firm and solid in appearance and smooth and compact in texture and on-the-month feel. The curd is cooked by slowly heating it to very high temperature for thirty to forty-five minutes. Some hard cheese in this classification may contain openings or eyes; think Emmental (a lot) and Comté (a few). The Swiss cheeses you are most familiar with would be the reigning champ here, boasting more air than cheese per slice.

The openings are mainly due to fermentation during the aging process; in some cheeses propionic bacteria is added to the milk during the make. This produces carbon dioxide, which creates gas bubbles which eventually pop, leaving the classic round openings. Cheese is constantly reinventing itself. It's never the same from day to day; microbiological processes are occurring all the time during the *affinage* (aging) of these cheeses.

The second branch of the hard cheese family tree is the extra-hard class, the "rock star" of this category being Parmigiano-Reggiano! Other classics are Pecorino and Piave Vecchio. These are referred to as *grana cheeses* (good for grating). Extra-hard cheese gets its hard body from its personal trainer, the cheesemaker. First, the cream from this milk is skimmed off to provide a lower fat content for the cheese. Because you have a lower fat content, drainage of moisture from the cheese curd will speed up. Small curd size is key, as it is easier for the moisture to be expelled from the curd. Then the curd is cooked to a very high temperature, between 48–54°C/118–129°F, removing even more moisture. Low moisture is the goal in hard cheese. It allows less enzymatic activity in the aging

RIGHT: Classic Swiss cheese with large mechanical eye openings.

RIGHT: Enjoy Parmigiano-Reggiano in a delicious new way. Taste its nutty, salty, and savory goodness when you pop a nugget into your mouth.

process, enabling the cheese to be preserved or aged out over a longer period of time.

The last part of the workout for the hard-cooked cheese category is (bench) pressing. Again, pressing the curd expels more moisture in the form of whey that was trapped between the curds. Pressing is key here, because pressing too much or too little will create a crumbly body in the cheese, not ideal for this type of cheese. Some cheese types in this family may be placed in a brine solution as part of the make process; for example Parmigiano-Reggiano is brined for up to twenty-one days. During the brining an exchange occurs. Salt is absorbed into the cheese, and whey is expelled from the cheese. Brining also helps create rind development, which allows for less cracking and longer aging time for this style of cheese. The continuous process of removing moisture for a longer maturation period will provide an excellent flavor profile for this extra-hard cheese category.

Next time you hit the cheese shop, give the classic extra-hard cheeses like Parmigiano-Reggiano and Pecorino Sardo, which are traditionally grated over pasta and salads, another try. Don't relegate them to being only for cooking. Taste their nutty, salty, and savory goodness when you pop a nugget into your mouth. The concentrated sweet flavor and nuances of grassy pastures in these cheeses are delightful. When you're done workin' out, pick up a young pinot noir and a few hard bodies and . . . rock on!

Blue cheese

The Blue cheese classification often sings the blues. In spite of its smoky, earthy, creamy goodness, inspired by the gorgeous blue and green veins that create its iconic appearance, it remains an underappreciated cheese category for consumers. Though this classification is a large family, they all have one thing in common—a blue mold commonly known as *Penicillium roqueforti*. The curd of this cheese is inoculated with strains

LEFT: Bayley Hazen Blue, Jasper Hill Farm, Greensboro, Vermont   PHOTO CREDIT: *Louis Polish*

of this mold or it is added to the milk during the make. Once the cheesemaking process is complete, the real changes to this family of cheese occur. A few days to a week after production the cheese is needled (piercing with long needles) to allow the introduction of air into the body of the cheese. Allowing oxygen to enter through these fine tunnels promotes the *Penicillium roqueforti* to do its dance, making its way along the narrow paths to the interior of the paste and creating the intricate pattern of bluish-green lines called *veining*.

Blue cheese is aged in very humid conditions to facilitate mold development and to prevent the cheese from drying out and cracking. Aging room average temperatures are 10°C/50°F with humidity at about 90 percent.

One of the best ways to appreciate and understand the differences between the cheeses in the Blue cheese family is to generalize them by texture or body composition. This ranges from creamy to firm with a crumbly body in the middle somewhere. The classic creamy Blues are soft-ripened with a bloomy rind made in the Danish style, like Cambozola and Danish Blue. They present a silky, supple taste on the mouth, the paste is sweeter, and the blue mold flavors are generally milder. This is a good style to start with if you are new to the Blues. You will find the firmer Blues are meatier, with a beefy, nutty flavor. The body is crumbly looking, and the paste is less ivory in color and more tan

Cheese to go
· · · · · · · · · · · · · · · · ·

Body Piercing Blues
Veining, needling, piercing—
yikes! Not very pretty-sounding
words but all essential to the
transformation of Blue cheese.
The body or format of the
cheese is aerated by the pro-
cess of piercing with long thin
needles. This can be done both
by hand and with a mechanical
press. Oxygen makes its way
down the tunnels, which
helps the
blue mold
flourish.

to golden. Try the French classic Fourme d'Ambert; it's creamy, mild, and very approachable. The final category in identifying different Blue cheeses within this family is the crumbly-creamy texture; many of the Blue cheeses in this style are produced in the United States. Generally, these Blues have a very thin rind and look moist, but the body will be firm, with lots of tiny craters of blue mold uniformly spread throughout the paste. Roquefort, the French classic, is a good example of this style of Blue; try a young Berkshire Blue made from Jersey cow's milk, Point Reyes Blue, or Rogue River Blue from the famed Rogue Creamery in Oregon.

Categories of Rind Development

Rind development is another wonder of cheesemaking, and proper rind development is key to the success of all cheese. All styles of cheese have a rind, though some go unseen and underappreciated. The whole idea behind the rind is to keep the delicious goodness of the cheese intact. The rind on a cheese works in two ways: as a buffer or guard against unwanted bacteria and mold that will compromise the cheese's interior and as a facilitator of the ripening of the cheese with the addition of good bacteria and molds. All rinds are a creation of aging, formed during this process of allowing the cheese to come to full ripened bliss.

Coulommiers

Petite Frere

Tomme de Savoie

Oma

Rind formation is due to the surface of the cheese drying and developing different types of microorganisms that will impart a wide spectrum of flavor and appearance characteristics to the cheese. When categorizing rinds into cheese families, think about the duality of the rind's role inside and outside the wedge!

LEFT: This runny, ripe Camembert is just begging for a French baguette to join the fun.

Bloomy-rind (1) soft-ripened

THE WINY RIND . . . JUST BEGGING TO BE EATEN

The standard by which you know this type of rind is a soft-ripened Camembert or Brie. Those cheeses are developed with the addition of the essential molds *Geotrichum candidum* and/or the slower-growing *Penicillium candidum* mold, either added to the milk during the make or sprayed on the cheese later in the aging process. The familiar white fuzzy texture you find on soft-ripened cheese, like Humboldt Fog from Cypress Grove and France's Bûcheron, is an example of a bloomy rind. These molds promote the creamy; ivory-colored; intricate patterns of mold growth. Check out the tapestry-like patterns found on a Saint-Marcellin from France or a Coupole from Vermont Butter and Cheese Creamery. In general the rind on these cheeses is edible and in many cases will impart flavor and texture to the overall on-the-mouth experience of the cheese.

Mixed-rind (2) washed and bloomy cheese

MIXED BLESSING OF A RIND . . .

A mixed-rind cheese has a few steps in the aging process that help develop the characteristic orangish-white rind you find on mixed-rind cheese such as the famed Raclette and Reblochon from France. The pro-

ABOVE: Coupole   PHOTO CREDIT: *Adeline Druart*

cess involves washing the cheeses' surface and allowing the mold to bloom on the rind. There is yeast already active in the green cheese (young cheese) when the process of washing the cheese with a smear solution begins. This helps to neutralize the surface of the cheese, which allows the *Brevibaterium linens*, known as *B. linens*, to develop on the surface of the rind, creating the orangish, sometimes reddish, color of the rind. Toward the end of the aging process, the washing stops, allowing the molds on the rind to then bloom and create the fluffy, white mold you see uniformly on the surface of the cheese.

Washed-rind (3) soft-ripened, semi-hard hard cheese

WASH AWAY THE BLOOM . . .

The category of washed-rind cheese is similar to that of the mixed rind in that washing occurs throughout the aging process. The blooming is held at bay, and mold is not allowed to bloom on the rind, keeping it in check through the smearing or washing process. The *B. linens* are allowed to do their thing, breaking down fat and protein, adding to the flavor profile of the cheese while imparting the distinctive orangish to pinkish surface color. The activity of all the yeast on the surface will create an aromatic cheese as well. This is sometimes off-putting to those unaware of the creamy, gooey goodness that lies beneath the rind. Try two of Vermont's best—Winnimere, from Jasper Hill Farm, and Twig Wheel, from Twig Farm—or the classic Livarot from France. The rind on washed-rind cheese is generally not consumed.

Natural-rind (4) semi-hard and hard cheese

NATURALLY YOURS . . .

The natural-rind cheese category is large. These are rinds that develop their exterior while in the aging room or cheese cave as the rind originates from the environment. At work on rind development are the natural flora and fauna present in the aging facility. As well, additional molds may be introduced either intentionally by the *affineur* (cheese finisher) or from commingling of molds from other cheeses being aged in the same area. Moisture levels, air circulation, and turning of the cheese are also important elements for natural rind development. One method of natural rind development is bandaging, wrapping the entire cheese with cloth and covering it with lard to seal in the moisture and protect it during the aging process. The bandage acts as a host for the mold to develop and create the natural rind. Stellar examples of this natural rind development are Cabot, Montgomery, and Keens clothbound cheddars. Natural-rind cheeses generally have earthy, musty, rustic aromas, imparted by where and how they are aged. Collectively, the cave climate and temperature, natural flora on the ground and in the air, moisture levels, and many more minute details at work in the cave all combine to develop the *terroir* of the cheese. This category has an amazing array of rind colors, from light grays to deeper blue hues. Some classics to identify

Cheese to go
· · · · · · · · · · · · · · ·

They're called washed-rind cheeses because as they mature, their rinds are rubbed or washed with a brine solution, usually a mixture of water and salt. Like the traditional *marc de Bourgogne* blend used to wash down Époisses, the brine encourages the growth of *Brevibacterium linens*, creating an orange surface of the rind. These good bacteria work to keep harmful bacteria at bay and to develop an earthy, meaty, sweet character in the cheese.

ABOVE: These natural-rind cheeses from the market in Rennes, Brittany, show a range of size and color found in natural-rind cheeses.

next time you're in the cheese shop are; Tomme de Savoie, with its deep charcoal gray rind, Stony Man from Everona Dairy, and the famed Spanish Garrotxa with its velvety blue-gray mold.

On the banks of Barton Creek, in Dripping Springs, Texas, a cheesemaker lives and works with her family on a farm known as Pure Luck. Famous for its certified organic culinary herbs and award-winning artisan goat cheeses, this farmstead has been home to its master cheesemaker Amelia Sweethardt and her family for decades. Having lived on the farm since the age of two, Amelia has witnessed the growth of Pure Luck from its humble beginnings of untilled pastures in 1979 to its successful present-day status as a certified organic culinary herb farm and commercial goat dairy.

The mastermind behind Pure Luck's origins and original successes was Amelia's mother, Sara Bolton. It was Sara who began the farm's first vegetable garden, and her love for goats and cheesemaking

led to the expansion of the farm in 1995 to include not only organic herbs and vegetables but also a commercial dairy. Sarah was also the one who first piqued Amelia's interest in cheesemaking. The down-to-earth Amelia was twenty years old when her mother asked her to return to the farm to help her make cheese. "She asked, so I did it," says Amelia, and she's been making cheeses ever since.

Although Sara died in 2005, the principles on which she built Pure Luck Farm still remain ingrained in each of the six family members of the Pure Luck Farm team. It's all about discerning quality. "We don't try to do anything new, but rather improve on the things that we already do to make them the best we can with a consistent quality. We don't overlook anything. If something is not right, then it is not right and we fix it."

From an early age, an organic lifestyle and hard work ethic were instilled in Amelia and her three sisters by her mother. "Growing up, everyone learned how to work. It was the best thing that my mother gave us, and it has always worked for us. However, I did always think that we had a disproportionate amount of chores compared to other people."

Besides the regular day-to-day chores around the farm, Amelia's mother would sometimes call on Amelia and her sister, Gitana, to milk the goats if she herself was unable to for one reason or another. As goats thrive on consistency, this wasn't as easy as it sounded. "The goats loved my mother and would do anything for her, but when my sister and I tried to milk them, we would sometimes end up chasing them around for an hour. When you chase them, goats just get farther and farther away from you and move faster and faster."

Amelia's hard work has paid off. She is now in charge of running Pure Luck Farm's flourishing cheese business and managing the goat herd. During their busiest season Amelia transforms 450 gallons of goat's milk into 600 pounds of the most delicious Chèvre, Blue, feta, Claire de Lune, Sainte Maure, and Del Cielo with the help of her husband, Ben, and her sister, Claire. She credits the seventy-two resident Nubian and Alpine goats for much of this success. "It starts with the animals. The cheese cannot get any better than the milk."

To make great cheese, Pure Luck's small crew raises healthy, well-cared-for goats. With fifty acres of fenced pasture to graze on and a barn to return home to when the weather or their desire necessitates, the goats are happy and reared naturally. Most farms give their animals access to pasture, but Pure Luck prides itself on giving their goats access to a barn. "The goats are let outside with the option to come back to the barn if they desire. They will all eventually come home. It's just like anyone wanting to be healthy and happy. We let them live as they please and give them the best life that we can." In return the goats reward Amelia with high-quality milk that allows her to make her six varieties of prize cheeses. "We are goat people. We know them and we love them."

Since Pure Luck's cheese plant is right on the farm's premises, Amelia is able to look out over the pasture and watch the goats as she works. "One of my favorite things to do is stand in front of one of the windows in the cheese plant wrapping cheese. You can really be there in the moment and not be thinking about the next thing. Being able to look out the windows at the view is really relaxing."

Pure Luck Farm offers six different cheeses and boasts many awards for their efforts. For now the buck stops in Austin, Texas, where they currently sell their cheese to local grocers and restaurants. With successes aplenty, you would think it would be a no-brainer for Pure Luck to expand their business. The thought on the farm, however, is quite the contrary. "We do what we do. Our market has grown with us, but we are not trying to grow. We are happy where we are." Pure Luck Farm remains a small farmstead on the banks of Barton Creek where a cheesemaker lives and works with her family.

Pure Luck Farm & Dairy
· ·

Owners: Amelia and Gitana Sweethardt, Claire and Hope Bolton
Cheesemakers: Amelia Sweethardt and Claire Bolton
Dripping Springs, Texas
E-mail: pureluck@purelucktexas.com
Website: www.purelucktexas.com

Texas Cheese Soufflé

A soufflé sounds sophisticated and complicated, but not this one. The soul of a soufflé resides in the egg whites. As in artisan cheesemaking, it takes an artful hand to bring them to just the right stiffness and to fold in gently. This is a wonderful make-ahead dish for a culinary convenient dinner! *Serves 6*

½ lb fresh goat Chèvre

4 large free-range eggs

3½ T unsalted butter

⅓ C all-purpose flour

1⅓ C milk (whole or 2 percent)

1 T Dijon mustard

1 T finely chopped herbs i.e. thyme, tarragon, basil

Approx. ½ tsp kosher salt and black pepper

Preheat oven to 375°F and butter 6 ¾-C. ramekins.

Separate the eggs.

In a medium saucepan, melt butter.

Whisk in flour and cook approximately 2–3 minutes over low heat, whisking.

Add milk, slowly, whisking in, bring to simmer, and cook 2–3 minutes, until sauce thickens. Remove pan from heat.

Whisk in egg yolks, mustard, thyme, cheese, and salt and pepper to taste.

In a mixer, beat whites with a pinch of salt until they just hold stiff peaks.

Fold in ⅓ of whites to lighten, and then gently fold in the rest of the whites.

Divide into the buttered ramekins.

Arrange them in a baking pan and pour hot water halfway up the sides.

Bake until slightly puffed and light golden brown.

Cool and turn upside down onto a buttered cookie sheet.

Can be refrigerated overnight.

When ready to serve, preheat oven to 375°F. Place soufflés in oven. Bake until heated through and slightly puffed. Turn soufflés over and out onto a plate of local mixed greens and serve with Red Onion Marmalade (page 23).

Try with . . .

PHOTO CREDIT: *Olivia Farnham*

Off the Vine: Try a 2008 Bonny Doon Vin Gris de Cigare from the famed Bonny Doon Vineyard, Santa Cruz, California. This rosé wine is lovely, with dry fruitiness of apple bloom, white cherry, and a hint of spearmint. It is a wonderfully clean complement to the cheese and Dijon in the soufflé.

Appetite for Ale: American wheat beers are a good choice for this dish as they tend to be light but full of grainy sweetness with a hint of lemon, a perfect match for the tangy goat cheese in the soufflé. Try Sierra Nevada Wheat Beer (Sierra Nevada Brewing Company, Chico, California) or Blackbéary Wheat (Long Trail Brewing Company, Bridgewater Corners, Vermont).

Red Onion Marmalade

The sweet caramelizing of red onions and currants along with some heat from the red pepper flakes and ginger make this a satisfying accompaniment to the Texas Cheese Soufflé, enhancing the golden goodness of baked eggs and tangy fresh Chèvre. *Makes 3 cups*

6 C peeled, sliced red onion	1 C light brown sugar
¼ C olive oil	¾ C red or cider vinegar
1½ T grated fresh ginger	2 T dry sherry
1 tsp red pepper flakes	½ C dried currants
½ T salt	

Heat oil in heavy, large pot over medium heat.

Add pepper flakes and onion, stir, cover, and cook on low heat till tender, stirring occasionally, about 15 minutes.

Add salt, brown sugar, vinegar, sherry, and ginger. Cook uncovered until onions are very tender and mixture is thick, stirring frequently, about 20 minutes.

Add currants and cook for another 5 minutes, stirring frequently.

Cool completely. Can be prepared 4 days ahead. Cover and refrigerate.

Note: This is a fantastic accompaniment to any cheese board.

PHOTO CREDIT: *Olivia Farnham*

❝ Andy and I have always approached cheesemaking with the understanding that our cheese will never be better than our milk, and for this reason we take a great effort to ensure that our raw material is as good as it can be. We are a quality-driven business, and quality begins with the way we produce and process our milk. Every cow in the herd is managed as an individual. Most important, we process the fantastic milk our herd of Ayrshire cows produces seven days a week, 365 days a year, because what's the sense in making the best milk in the State of Vermont and just letting it sit, losing the very character we are trying to express? ❞

—MATEO KEHLER, Jasper Hill Farm / Cellars at Jasper Hill

② Milk Composition and Seasonality

MILK REPRESENTS different things to different people. For the kid eating Oreos, it's a place to dunk a few, and for the mom shopping for groceries, it's a gallon of white liquid in a plastic jug with a handle. For a cheesemaker, it's a very different thing. Milk is the raw material used for making cheese. It's the answer to an age-old question "How can we preserve milk?" Cheese is the answer; it is a value-added product you produce on the farm. Understanding the composition and seasonality of milk is key to making this wondrous product; you simply cannot make good cheese from bad milk. Milk is a complicated substance. Technically it is an opaque liquid produced by mammals and consumed for nutritious reasons. The lactation cycle of the animal plays a big role in milk production and seasonality. The most common milk used in the United States is cow's milk. A cow generally produces milk for ten months out of the year, with a gestation cycle of about nine months. Sixty days or so prior to the birth of a calf, cows are no longer milked and are "dried off." In general the lactation cycles are about 309 days for a cow, 277 for a goat, and 180 days for a sheep.

MILK COMPOSITION

The milk contains four major components; water, lactose (milk sugar), lipids (fat), and proteins; minor components are the minerals, trace elements, and vitamins.

Water: Milk is 87 percent water and 13 percent solids. The main goal of a cheesemaker is to concentrate the milk solids by different techniques in order to make cheese. The amount of moisture (water) left in the cheese food matrix will have a tremendous impact on the cheese's shelf life. As a general rule of thumb, the more moisture left in the cheese, the shorter the shelf life of the cheese will be. For example, the shelf life of soft cheese (e.g. Camembert) from the date of manufacture is usually about two months because this type of cheese usually contains a high amount of water. If you look at a hard cheese such as Comté, the shelf life from the date of manufacture can be a year or more.

Lactose: The lactose (the sugar in milk) will be used by different microorganisms added to the milk, such as lactic acid bacteria (starter culture). The lactic acid bacteria will transform the lactose into lactic acid, carbon dioxide (gas), and/or flavoring (diacetyl).

Lipids or butterfat: Fat globules and the small proteins contribute to the opaque white color of milk. The fat globules contain some yellow-orange carotene, enough in some breeds (such as Jersey cattle) to impart a golden tint to the milk. The milk fat will be extremely important, because the triglycerides that constitute 98 percent of the milk fat are going to be broken down and will free some fatty acids during the cheese-aging process, which will lead to the development of aromatic flavor compounds.

Proteins/Casein: Milk proteins consist of two important components, whey proteins and caseins. The caseins are the most important proteins for the cheesemaker because they are responsible for the organization of an organic net when making cheese. This is the main component responsible for the transformation of the milk from a liquid form to a gel. The whey proteins will be mainly lost in the whey at the draining-off stage of the cheesemaking process.

Different species of animals produce different milk quality.

Composition of 1 liter of whole cow's milk

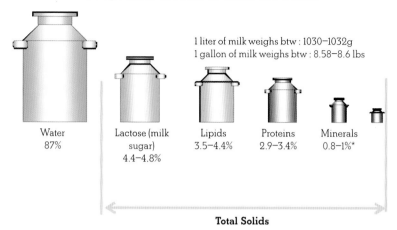

1 liter of milk weighs btw : 1030−1032g
1 gallon of milk weighs btw : 8.58−8.6 lbs

| Water 87% | Lactose (milk sugar) 4.4−4.8% | Lipids 3.5−4.4% | Proteins 2.9−3.4% | Minerals 0.8−1%* | |

Total Solids

* Some other elements in very small quantity—Among the most important are vitamins A and B

Most Common Cow Breeds

HOLSTEIN   **BROWN SWISS**   **JERSEY**

Composition	Holstein (%)	Brown Swiss (%)	Jersey (%)
Fat	3.4	3.86	5.05
Protein	3.3	3.48	3.79
Lactose	4.89	5.09	5.00
Total solids	12.26	13.15	14.54
Water	87.74	86.85	85.46

PHOTO CREDIT: *Sara Forest*

Composition of 1 liter of goat's milk

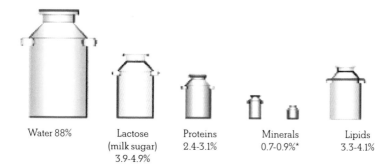

| Water 88% | Lactose (milk sugar) 3.9-4.9% | Proteins 2.4-3.1% | Minerals 0.7-0.9%* | Lipids 3.3-4.1% |

* Some other elements in very small quantity

Goat's milk and cow's milk are slightly different. The percentage of lipids (fat) is almost the same, but the fat globules from goat's milk are generally smaller, which makes the fat rise to the surface much more slowly than the fat from cow's milk. Furthermore, the fat in goat's milk doesn't contain any carotenes, which is why goat's-milk cheese tends to have a whiter cheese paste than cow's-milk cheese. Regarding the protein content, goat's milk on average contains less protein than cow's milk, which tends to decrease the cheesemaking yield.

Sheep's milk is higher in solids, fat, protein, lactose, and minerals than cow's milk, even that from Jersey cows, which is known to be higher in these values.

Composition of 1 liter of sheep's milk

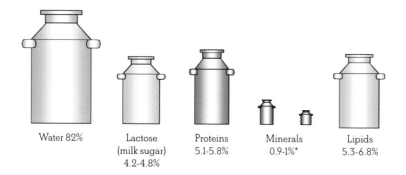

| Water 82% | Lactose (milk sugar) 4.2-4.8% | Proteins 5.1-5.8% | Minerals 0.9-1%* | Lipids 5.3-6.8% |

* Some other elements in very small quantity

The breeding and the feeding of the animals affects milk composition. Different breeds of animals produce different amounts of milk and milk of varying composition. As we can see in the table below, the protein and fat content will differ depending on the breed of cow being milked. Protein and fat content are the most important components in milk, and approximately 90 percent will end up in the final cheese.

MILK SELECTION: As the cheesemaker you will select a type of milk that will best suit the kind of cheese you're making.

Examples of milk protein/fat ratios for different families of cheese:

Cheese family	Cheese example	Protein/Fat ratio
Fresh cheese	Feta	0.9 to 0.95
	Mozzarella	1.2 to 1.25
Soft cheese	Camembert	0.86 to 0.93
	Muenster	0.85 to 0.9
Semi-hard cheese	Gouda	1 to 1.1
	Brick	1 to 1.05
Hard	Cheddar	0.9 to 1
	Swiss	1.15 to 1.2

The right milk protein/fat ratio is an essential key for cheesemaking. It will allow cheesemakers to control the intensity of the drainage of the cheese curds. The physicochemical components and the microbiological of milk are equally important for cheesemaking.

FACTORS AFFECTING MILK QUALITY

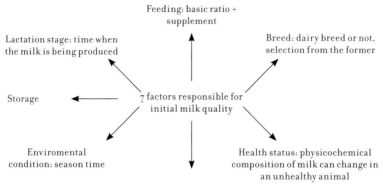

Feeding: basic ratio +
supplement

Lactation stage: time when
the milk is being produced

Breed: dairy breed or not,
selection from the former

Storage

7 factors responsible for
initial milk quality

Enviromental
condition: season time

Health status: physicochemical
composition of milk can change in
an unhealthy animal

Milking: different milking
methods and the risk of
microbiological contamination

Once you have selected your milk source, you are ready to start the basic cheesemaking steps.

AN OVERVIEW OF THE SEVEN STEPS IN THE CHEESEMAKING PROCESS

1. The first step in the process is adjusting the milk to the correct temperature the cheese make calls for. This may require warming up or cooling down the milk.

2. The second step in the process is to add starter culture (good bacteria) to the milk. The starter culture produces acid in the milk/cheese and develops flavor in the cheese.

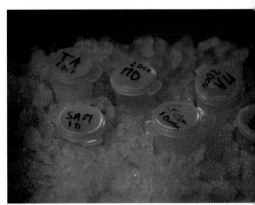

3. The third step in the process has a lot going on: coagulation, cutting, and stirring of the cheese. Adding coagulant will cause the milk to go from a liquid to semisolid state. The first real change you will see in the process is that the gel starts to firm up. Cutting with a cheese harp and stirring the curd come next in process.

4. The fourth step in the process is molding the cheese curd. The shape and size of your cheese will depend on the mold selection. Molding also allows for additional drainage of the whey.

5. The fifth step in the process is pressing the cheese. Pressing is done for varying lengths of time and with different weights. This allows the molded curds additional time to express more whey.

6. The sixth step in the process is salting the cheese. This step will express more whey from the cheese, helps with rind formation, adds flavor, and improves shelf life.

7. The seventh step in the process is aging. In this last step in the cheesemaking process, aging will help the cheese develop character and a flavor profile. During this step, many special adaptations can be made to the cheese, such as needling, smearing, brushing, waxing, and bandaging.

⚘ BONNIEVIEW FARM ⚘

The State of Vermont has the highest number of artisan cheesemakers per capita in the United States. One farm in particular has made a name for itself among the many and has become quite well known for its award-winning cheeses.

Bonnieview Farm is nestled in Vermont's Northeast Kingdom and offers stunning views of Mount Mansfield and the surrounding farm country, including many smaller farms and farmsteads as far as the eye can see. In the Urie family for more than a century, Bonnieview is the quintessential family dairy, not only because of its rich ancestral history but also because of the strong family spirit evident there today. The farm is currently owned by Neil Urie, who lives there with his wife, Kristin, their oldest oldest daughter, triplets (two daughters and a son), 200 sheep, two cows, two pigs, a flock of hens, a dog, a cat, and a llama. Everyone gets involved. "It is so wonderful to watch our oldest daughter Tressa bottle-feeding the baby lambs or chasing and catching chickens. She is really learning her way around the farm."

The birthplace of both Neil's grandfather and father, this 400-acre farm, ripe with pastures, fields, and forests, has spent most of its years as a commercial cow dairy. Neil became the fourth-generation Urie to run the property when he purchased it from his uncle in 1995. Just a few years later, in 1999, he transitioned it from a cow to a sheep dairy. "I transitioned from cows to sheep because of the variability of the milk pricing for the cows' milk. I was tired of the price of milk always fluctuating." This is when Neil began making cheese.

Known for his award-winning Mossend Blue, which took second place in 2007 from the American Cheese Society, Neil also makes Coomersdale, which placed second in its category in 2008 from the ACS competition. It is a sweet, nutty cheese made using a recipe from shepherds in the Pyrenees mountains; Ben Nevis, made from the same recipe, but hand-pressed with a unique shape and size; and a flavorful, fresh ewe's feta. Made in the small cheese house across the dirt road from their home, these four cheeses are all made from raw sheep's milk. "We don't do anything fancy with our cheeses, but we use a high-quality raw milk. Raw milk makes a better cheese." Working with three full-time interns, who live in the farm's yurt, and every once in a while receiving assistance from Tressa, Neil makes 8,000–10,000 pounds of sheep's-milk cheese each year from May to October.

The flock of resident sheep provides the milk for Bonnieview's cheese. Milked twice daily, these sheep spend their time feeding and lounging about in rotating pastures. After each milking, the sheep are led to a different area to ensure that they get the best, most lush grass available to them. "We do not use any chemicals in the pastures, so there are no health risks with the raw milk in that way," explained Kristin. It takes a full three weeks to rotate through all the pastures. During the on-pasture time, all the sheep are accompanied by their friend, Moon, Bonnieview's very own llama. Moon serves as the sheep's security, protecting them from coyotes and other wild animals. "Llamas have a fierce

ABOVE: Cheese reference: Coomersdale.

spit that will defend against unwanted visitors and keep the sheep safe," said Kristin.

In addition to cheesemaking, the farm also sells eggs; organic, hormone-free meat; bread baked in an outdoor clay oven; and wool products. Bonnieview's mission is to bring healthy food to the local community and offer people a connection to the source of their food. "We produce most of the food our family eats. If we don't, then we know the people who do." At one point, they butchered one of their cows, Roscoe, and were unsure of how to break the news to their three-year-old. But she took the information from the barn with aplomb, walking into the house and announcing, "Roscoe's in the freezer!"

Bonnieview's cheeses are sold at local farmers' markets and grocers, and they can be found in shops and restaurants throughout New England and New York.

Even with all that is currently going on at Bonnieview, Neil is still looking to grow. He hopes to increase his number of sheep and bring the farm back to its roots by bringing in more cows. With Tressa learning her way around the farm and three smaller ones coming up behind, Bonnieview should remain in the Urie family for many more generations to come.

PHOTO CREDIT: *Olivia Farnham*

Bonnieview Farm
· ·

Owner and cheesemaker: Neil & Kristin Urie
Craftsbury Common, Vermont
E-mail bonniecheese@gmail.com
Website: www.bonnieview.org

PHOTO CREDIT: *Louis Polish*

Mossend Blue Cheese Scalloped Potatoes

Adapted from recipe by Lee Duberman, Ariel's Restaurant

To ward off the winter blues, try making this savory, rich potato dish with your favorite local Blue cheese. Ours is from the family farm of Bonnieview in the heart of Vermont's lush Green Mountains. The layered look of a tower of cheesy goodness can be achieved by cutting the cooled potatoes with a baker's biscuit cutter. *Serves 8–10*

3 lbs Yukon Gold potatoes, peeled and thinly sliced	6 oz crumbled Blue cheese (Mossend Blue)
1½ C heavy cream	2 tsp kosher salt
1 C whole milk	1 T ground black pepper
3 T flour	4–5 sprigs of fresh thyme

Preheat oven to 350°F.

Butter bottom of a 12x16 baking dish (brownie or lasagna size).

Combine cream, milk, flour, salt, and pepper in a large bowl, mixing well. Add potato slices and mix well. Let soak for 12–15 minutes.

Layer the potato slices in the baking pan, placing crumbled Blue cheese between layers. Pour cream mixture over potatoes; push down so potatoes are all covered with sauce. Cover with aluminum foil,

Place in oven and bake, approx. 1 hour or until the potatoes are tender when pierced with a knife.

Uncover pan and approximately cook about 15 minutes longer until potatoes are allow to brown.

Cool for at least 1 hour before cutting into squares. Optional cut; use a round biscuit cutter for a mini potato tower (as seen in the photo). Reheat just before serving.

Try with . . .

Off the Vine: You will likely be serving this dish with the red meat of your choice, so a Cabernet Sauvignon would be a delightful choice. Cabs range from medium-bodied to full-bodied and are characterized by their high tannin content, which serves to provide structure and will stand up well to this rich potato dish. Try a McManis Family Vineyards Cabernet Sauvignon 2005.

Appetite for Non-ale: Hard apple cider has balanced flavors and substantial complexity. A perfect trifecta of sweetness, acidity, and tannin characteristics, needed to balance the fats in this cheesy dish. The drink is full-bodied, so it isn't overpowered by the cream and Blue cheese. Try Woodchuck Draft Cider (Middlebury, Vermont), Farnum Hill Ciders (New Hampshire), or Wyder's Cider (Northern California).

" As fresh milk is the body and soul of dairy products, the
starter culture is the beating heart of any fermented dairy
product. By choosing the right culture, treating it with care,
and using it properly in the manufacturing process, it will make
the difference between an ordinary dairy product and a superb
dairy delight that will encourage your customers to come back
again and again. So choose your cultures carefully, handle with
care, and create a cultured 'work of art' that will set you apart
from the rest. "

—STEVE FUNK, Cargill Texturizing Solutions, North America

③
Starter Cultures

THE FIRST STEP IN CHEESEMAKING is ripening the milk, when milk sugar (lactose) is converted to lactic acid. This is achieved by adding microorganisms (starter culture) to the milk. Increasing the acid in the milk will aid in the explosion of whey from the curd, help the rennet coagulate the milk, and make sure that the microbial flora will be sufficient for a good acidification and curing process during *affinage* (aging of the cheese). Starter culture also influences the development of the flavor profile in the cheese, pay close attention that it is healthy and active during the cheesemaking process. We teach that the quality of the milk must be exceptional, but a healthy starter culture is essential to good quality cheese as well. As Steve Funk indicates, it the "beating heart" of the cheese you are creating. The care and proper selection of starter culture will make the difference between an ordinary product and a superior one.

Milk ripening will vary depending on starter culture selection and the temperature and duration of the milk-heating process. Use your cheese recipe or make sheet as guidelines for these temperatures and the correct method of heating the milk.

When the milk reaches the required temperature, the starter culture is added. Remember the starter contains lactic acid–producing bacteria that will work to ripen (acidify) the milk. The timing on this will vary but it generally takes 30–60 minutes. Timing for the acidification of the milk is key; ripening must proceed at the proper rate. We control this process by planning the ripening time so that the level of lactic acid is exact. If there is too much acid in the production, the cheese will leak whey and sour during the aging process. Too little acid production could mean defects like gas holes caused by yeast or coliform bacteria contamination or a low flavor profile.

In this chapter, we will review how to choose different types of starter cultures for the different cheese families, their functions, and the variables necessary for best results.

Adding Starter Culture

There are two distinct types of microorganisms used during cheesemaking, *mesophilic* and *thermophilic* starter cultures. The mesophilic culture is a moderate-temperature-loving starter that generally grows best when the temperature is 25–30°C (77–86°F) with a maximum temperature of 40°C (104°F); anything above this will destroy the bacteria.

The thermophilic culture is a high-heat-loving starter used in cheese production where the curd is cooked and generally grows best when the temperatures is 35–40°C (95–107°F) with a maximum growth temperature of 60°C (140°F).

Examples of various starter cultures used for different cheese technologies:

Type	New name	Products
Mesophilic	Lactococcus lactis ssp cremoris	Fresh cheeses, Cheddar
	Lactococcus lactis ssp lactis	Feta, mimolette
	Lactococcus lactis ssp cremoris	Soft Cheeses
	Lactococcus lactis ssp lactis	Pressed Cheeses
	Leuconostoc mesenteroides spp cremoris	
	Lactococcus lactis	
	Lactococcus lactis ssp cremoris	Butter
	Lactococcus lactis ssp lactis	
	Lactococcus lactis ssp lactis biovar diacetylactis	
Thermophilic	Streptocossus salivarius ssp thermophilus	Yoghurt
	Lactobacillus delbrueckii ssp bulgaricus	Mozzarella
	Lactobacillus helveticus	Emmental
	Lactobacillus delbruekii ssp lactis	Comté

There are two subcategories of start cultures, which are referred to as homofermentative and heterofermentative starters.

The main goal of the homofermentative starter culture is to change the lactose (natural milk sugar) present in the milk, which is made up of one molecule of glucose and one molecule of galactose, into lactic acid. This produces a small amount of aromatic compounds, which will enhance the smell of the cheese. Homofermentative bacteria is mainly used for acid development in the cheese.

Heterofermentative starter culture changes the lactose into a small amount of lactic acid and a lot of aromatic compounds. Their main function is to enhance the flavor of the cheese.

An example of a heterofermentative starter bacteria is *Lactococcus ssp. lactis biovar diacetylactis*. When added to milk it is responsible for the production of diacetyl (which will develop a nutty flavor in the cheese). In addition to the lactic acid and the different aromatic compounds produced by the starter culture, the lactic acid bacteria also bring some enzymatic activity to the aging process of the cheese. Enzymes generated by the starter culture will help to break down the structure of the cheese, allowing it to become more liquid over time. A good example of this enzymatic activity in a finished cheese product would be a very ripe Camembert or Brie cheese. When you slice the cheese, it's runny, and the paste oozes out. Enzymes also help with flavor and aroma development.

Properties of Mesophilic Starter Culture

Mesophilic starter cultures are microorganisms that have an optimum growth temperature between 25°C/77°F and 30°C/86°F. Most mesophilic starter cultures will have a maximum temperature ranging from 39°C/102°F to 40°C/104°F. Any temperatures above the maximum growth temperature starts to inactivate most of the microorganisms. The maximum temperature requirements show why a combination of mesophilic and thermophilic starter cultures is needed when making a semi-cooked or cooked cheese.

Mesophilic starter culture is used for a large spectrum of cheeses, ranging from soft to hard cheeses.

Properties of Thermophilic Starter Culture

Thermophilic starter culture bacteria have an optimum growth temperature ranging from 35°C/95°F and 45°C/113°F. Their maximum temperature is usually about 60°C/140°F. The thermophilic bacteria generally are used in making cooked cheese due to their high temperature resistance. Nowadays, some strains of thermophilic starter cultures are used in the manufacturing process of pressed, non-cooked cheese and soft cheeses. Even some strains of thermophilic cultures, when not in their optimum temperature environment, can be used for the production of a substance called exopolysaccharide (EPS). So for example, the use of TA050 from Danisco will produce some EPS, creating a creamy texture for soft cheeses, holding the cheese paste together and preventing it from becoming too runny.

Measuring starter culture:

STEP 1: A two-decimal scale is required to be accurate.

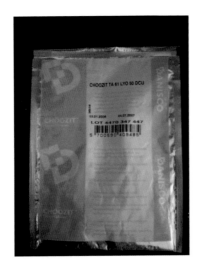

STEP 2: Locate amount of starter DCU in sample bag (example the bag contains 50 DCU).

STEP 3: Take a sterile container. (When I say sterile, I mean take a brand-new vial.)

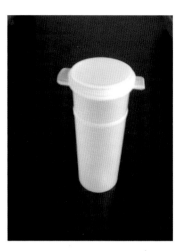

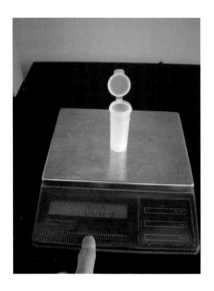

STEP 4: Place empty container on the scale. Zero out scale.

STEP 5: Transfer all the starter culture from the bag into the container and record how much it weighs. (The weight of the starter culture in the bag is 8.44g).

STEP 6: Now that we know how much 50 DUC weighs, we need to calculate how much 1 DCU weighs. In step 2, the bag of starter culture contained 50 DCU. In step 5 the starter culture weighs 8.44g, meaning 50 DCU weighs 8.44g in our example. In order to find out how heavy 1 DCU is, we need to divide 8.44 by 50.
8.44/50 = 0.17g
This means that 1 DCU weighs 0.17g.

STEP 7: Record this information on the bag. You don't want to lose it. Once the bag is open, it will be impossible to define how much DCU weighs.

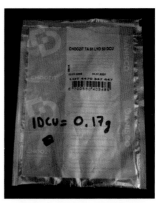

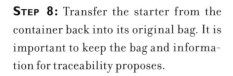

STEP 8: Transfer the starter from the container back into its original bag. It is important to keep the bag and information for traceability proposes.

Weigh the empty bag, and keep this information for your records. The weight of the empty bag won't change over time.
The next time that you receive a new bag of starter culture, you just have to weigh it and the content together and remove the weight of the bag.
Example: The bag empty weighs 4g, the bag with the starter culture weight 12.44g.
You will remove 4g from the 12.44g (12.44 – 4 = 8.44g).
Now you know how much the starter culture weighs in the bag, without transferring to the container.

Weighing Starter Culture in Production: More than 20 Gallons of Milk

A: Look at what your recipe or make sheet calls for:

Milk		100 L/26.45Gal
Lactococcus lactis ssp. lactis bio diacetylactis	MD99	0.5 DCU
Streptococcus salivarius ssp. thermophilus	TA061	3 DCU

B: Figure out how many DCU you will need based on the volume of milk that you have.

Example: If we have 51 gallons of milk in our vat, how many DCU of TA061 are we going to need?

3 DCU   26.45 gallons

? DCU   51 gallons

? DCU = (3 * 51) / 26.45

? DCU = 5.78 DCU

With 51 gallons we will need to use 5.78 DCU of the TA061.

C: Now, we need to figure out to how much those 5.78 DCU weigh.

In step 7 in the procedure above, we wrote on the bag that 1 DCU = 0.17g

In order to figure how much starter to weigh, we need to multiply 0.17 by 5.78 (0.17*5.78 = 0.98g).

It means that for the amount of milk that we have, we need to measure 0.98g of the TA061.

> Homestead cheesemakers tend to use the same volume of milk each make. Filling sterile containers with 45.6 ml of Parmalat® starter-culture milk and freezing them in your freezer would help save time. For the next make, thaw the solution under cold tap water and use it right away in the cheesemaking process.

Weighing Starter Culture in Production: Less than 20 Gallons of Milk

It is difficult to properly measure the amount of dry starter culture needed for a small amount of milk for cheese production. Here is a foolproof trick to help with accuracy.

STEP 1: Follow the steps indicated above up to step 8. Measure 1000ml of UHT Parmalat® (UHT is shelf-stable milk found next to the non-refrigerated soy milk; be sure it is UHT milk). You can also use UHT skim or 2 percent reduced-fat milk. With a clean and sanitized measuring cylinder, transfer the milk to a sanitized container and place it in an ice water bath. Add 12.5 DCU of starter culture to the milk and mix well (make sure to use a clean and sanitized spoon to stir).

STEP 2: Check amount the recipe calls for and figure out how many DCU you will need based on the volume of milk you have.

	Commercial name	Milk quantity 100liters/26.45gallons
Lactococcus lactis ssp. lactis bio diacetylactis	MD99	0.5 DCU
Streptococcus salivarius ssp. thermophilus	TA061	3 DCU

Example: If we have 5 gallons of milk in our vat, how many DCU of TA061 are we going to need?

3 DCU   26.45 gallons

? DCU   5 gallons

? DCU = (3 * 5) / 26.45

? DCU = 0.57 DCU

With 5 gallons we will need to use 0.57 DCU of the TA061.

STEP 3: We now know that we need 0.57 DCU of the TA061 for the 5 gallons of milk that we have in our cheese vat. We also know that we have mixed 12.5 DCU of starter culture with 1000 ml of UHT Parmalat® milk. Now we need to calculate how many milliliter of Parmalat® milk we need order to have 0.57 DCU of starter culture.

12.5 DCU   1000 ml

0.57 DCU   ? ml

? DCU = (0.57 * 1000) / 12.5

? DCU = 45.6 ml

So you will need to measure 45.6 ml of Parmalat® starter-culture milk for 5 gallons of milk.

Equipment	Description	URL
Scale with 2 decimals	American Weigh BT2–201 Digital Gram Pocket Grain Jewelry Scale 200 x 0.01g	www.amazon.com
Sterile plastic vials	LDPE Sample Vials	www.usplastic.com
pH meter	Thermo Orion 2-Star Benchtop pH Meter	www.nelsonjameson.com
Buffer solution	500 ml pH buffer 4.01 and 7.0	www.nelsonjameson.com
Delicate wipers	Kimtech Science Kimwipes	www.nelsonjameson.com
Wash bottle	Safety labeled wash bottles	www.nelsonjameson.com

Adding Starter Culture

Once you have determined the amount of starter culture needed and properly measured it out, evenly distribute the starter culture into the warm milk. The milk temperature should be within the parameters required to activate the starter. Once the starter cultures have been added to the milk, stir gently to distribute evenly in the milk. Once the culture is stirred in, do not mix for the remainder of the ripening time. Excessive agitation reduces the rate of acidification and could lead to damage of fat globules.

Calibrate and Use of pH Meter

STEP 1: Start by rinsing the temperature and pH probe with the wash water bottle and then delicately dry the probes with the Kimwipes® paper.

STEP 2: Place probes in the 7.0 pH buffer solution and press the button "calibrate." The message "pH Cal" should appear on the pH meter screen. The calibration of the pH 7.0 buffer solution is considered finished when the pH signal stops blinking.

Step 3: Do not remove the probes from the pH buffer solution 7.0. Press the button "calibrate" again. The message CAL. Two should appear on the bottom of the screen. The message "pH Cal" should appear on the pH meter screen. Remove the probes from the solution and rinse them with the wash water bottle. Dry the probes with the Kimwipes® paper, and put the probes in the pH buffer solution 4.01. When the pH signal stops blinking, the calibration is finished. Press the measure button and a sign SLP should appear on the bottom of the screen. SLP means slope. The slope of the calibration should always be equal or above 95 percent.

Step 4: Once the calibration is complete, rinse the probes with the wash water bottle, dry the probes with the Kimwipes® paper, and then put the probes in the milk sample and press "measure." The numbers 4 and 7 should appear on the screen to indicate that the pH meter has been calibrated.

Step 5: When you are ready to check pH measurement of the milk, plunge the pH and temperature probes in your milk sample and press "measure." Wait until the pH probe signal stops blinking and read the pH value. Remove the probes from the sample, rinse them, and put back their storage cap.

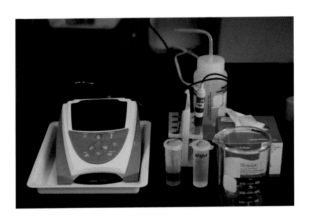

Checking Starter Culture Activity

The best way to check the starter culture activity is to monitor the acidification of the milk/cheese over time. In most of the different cheese technology the acidification (pH change) will occur during the drainage of the cheese curd. The best way to monitor the pH change is to record different pH values at different times during cheesemaking and between different batches.

ABOVE An example of a bloomy-rind cheese

Example of pH value in a soft bloomy-rind cheese

Step	Time (min)	Reference pH values	Actual pH values
Milk	0	6.70 (± 0.05)	6.72
Starter addition	20	6.50 (± 0.05)	6.52
Coagulant addition	65	6.45 (± 0.05)	6.5
Cutting	95	6.40−6.45 (± 0.05)	6.42
Hooping (molding)	120	6.30 (± 0.05)	6.25
Hooping + 1H	180	6.00 (± 0.05)	6.01
Hooping + 3H	300	5.70 (± 0.05)	5.65
Hooping + 5H	420	5.45 (± 0.05)	5.43
Hooping + 8H	600	5.10 (± 0.05)	5.05
De-hooping (remove from the mold)	1080	4.90 (± 0.05)	4.95

The best way to compare the acid development between batches is to plot the pH values and to compare the values from batch to batch.

Example of acid development from batch to batch:

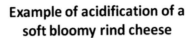

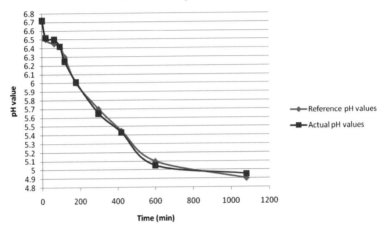

Preventing Starter Culture Failure

Different factors can affect the activity of your starter culture.

First, make sure to follow the manufacturer's instructions for the best handling and storage of the culture. Most of the starter cultures available for home or small cheesemakers are freeze-dried starter culture. Those type of cultures usually need to be kept at a maximum temperature of 4°C/39°F (your regular freezer) in order to keep a shelf life of 18 months from the date of production. Using starter that has been stored inadequately and/or expired can result in a lack of acid production during the cheesemaking process.

The second cause of starter failure is due to bacteriophage (phage) attack from your cheesemaking environment. Phage is little viruses present in your cheesemaking environment that are able to slow down and/or stop the activity of your starter culture. The best way to prevent phage attack is to ask your starter culture supplier for the proper rotation of starter culture needed in order to prevent phage attack. For example, the best starter alternative rotation for the MA 011 from Danisco would be MA 014, MA 016, and MA 019. This means that every three to five days, you will have to switch between the different MA starter cultures. The rotation of the starter culture won't change your acidification pattern and/or the flavor of the product that you are trying to make, but it will prevent phage attack.

A third cause for starter failure could be microbiological contamination, which can have a major impact on your starter culture activity. Microbial contaminants compete with starter cultures for food, overtaking the process. This often leads to a slower acidification pattern. Contaminants can come from poor hand washing and insufficient cleaning of the cheesemaking equipment and environment.

Convertion of DCU from Danisco /Unit from Chr. Hansen /percentage of bulk starter culture

Most of the traditional dairy books recommend the use of 1 percent of mesophilic starter culture as an example. The 1 percent of mesophilic starter culture represents 1 percent (v/v) of bulk starter culture. It usually doesn't say if the starter culture is made of homofermentative and/or heterofermentative bacteria. I would recommend contacting a starter culture supplier and asking him or her what type of starter culture he or she would recommend based on the type of cheese that you are trying to make.

The general rule of thumb is to use 1 percent of bulk starter culture, the equivalent of 6.25 DCU of starter culture from Danisco or 10 Units from Chr. Hansen.

EXAMPLE: If a dairy book recommends using 1 percent of mesophilic starter culture for the manufacturing process of cheese, you would use 6.25DCU of MA011, MA014, MA016, or MA019 from Danisco or 10 Units from Series R600.

Starter Culture Suppliers

Company name	URL
Dairy Connection	www.dairyconnection.com
Danlac Canada	www.danlac.com
Fromagex	www.fromagex.com
Glengarry Cheese and Dairy Supply	www.glengarrycheesemaking.on.ca
Kelley Supply	www.kelleysupply.com
Leeners	www.leeners.com
Lehmans	www.lehmans.com
New England cheesemaking Supply	www.cheesemaking.com

"I grew up with the saying 'if we couldn't grow it, we couldn't eat it,'" said Gianaclis Caldwell, master cheesemaker and co-owner of Pholia Farm in Rogue River, Oregon. This do-it-yourself attitude stuck with her over the years and is not only apparent in the way she and her husband, Vern, run the farm but also was the motivation that got her started making goat cheese in the first place. "We wanted to make our own dairy products using our own milk."

In 2003, the family was living on enough land to consider adding a milking animal to their small hobby farm in San Diego County. "I wanted to make my own sour cream. You couldn't recycle the plastic containers that the sour cream came in and how can you live without sour cream?" After some research, she found that Nigerian Dwarf Goats would be a better way to go. "I was a typical cow person. I was a snob about goats." She found that her two girls would be able to handle the smaller goats much more easily, making it no trouble to get them involved.

So, with goat's milk at the ready, Gianaclis began reading up on how to make goat cheese and learned how to do it from Ricki Carroll's book *Home Cheese Making*. "Growing up on a farm we did almost everything ourselves. If you needed something done, you would learn how to do it. It brings a lot of empowerment."

Chèvre and mozzarella were the first cheeses Gianaclis experimented with, along with some homemade yogurt followed by feta and finally hard cheeses. In 2006, three years after she taught herself how to make cheese, the family began selling it under the name Pholia Farm. "When you have a goat-breeding farm, you have to come up with a completely unique name for it, one that has not already been used." She and her husband decided to name the farm using a combination of their two daughter's names, *Phoebe* and *Amelia*.

In 2005, Gianaclis and Vern moved their family back to Oregon, where they bought twenty-four acres of land, part of the same property where Gianaclis grew up. This is where they decided to build their off-grid home and farm powered by solar panels and a small microhydro-electric turbine, with hot water and radiant flooring provided by a high efficiency/low emissions indoor wood boiler along with solar hot water panels. "We are off the grid by choice. We're not as remote as it seems; we could get power up here. We just choose not to. We like being responsible for our own consumption. We try to live very conscientiously."

Today, Pholia Farm sells five different varieties of aged raw-milk goat cheese all named after mountains or points of interest in the Rogue River area, except for their Special Seedy. They make two on a regular basis—Elk Mountain and Hillis Peak, which are aged for at least six months—as well as three seasonal styles, Special Seedy, Wimer Winter, and Covered Bridge. They make 200–300 pounds of cheese per month. "It's great to work with Vern. We get to talk about pH and acidity and all the romantic cheesy things a couple talks about."

BELOW: Gianaclis in the aging room.

ABOVE: Pholia Farm.

Gianaclis's cheesemaking knowledge and business have grown over the past five years and so has the family's goat herd. Although the Caldwells swore they would never keep more than six does and no bucks when they first started out, the farm is now home to around 85 goats, including 12 males. With no grazing pastures on their farm, only forest, one of the family members and the goats go on a goat walk when the weather permits, which allows the goats to browse and gives them good exercise. Not only does this help to make the milk more flavorful, but it keeps the goats in shape for showing as well.

"Improving our breed and our herd name is just as important as improving our cheese." The goats at Pholia Farm are shown in national competitions by Gianaclis and their youngest daughter, Amelia, and have won many awards.

Hoping to encourage new cheesemakers and help them find answers to many of the questions facing those going into this business, Gianaclis has written *The Farmstead Creamery Advisor: The Complete Guide to*

ABOVE: Hillis Peak.

Building and Running a Small Farm-Based Cheese Business (Chelsea Green Publishing, Vermont). You can find Pholia Farm cheeses at a few cheese counters in the United States or at the farm.

Pholia Farm
· ·

Owner and cheesemaker: Gianaclis Caldwell
Evans Creek, Rogue River, Oregon
E-mail: contact@oregoncheeseguild.org
Website: www.pholiafarm.com

Quinoa Salad with Sautéed Cauliflower, Bacon, and Chèvre

PHOTO CREDIT: *Olivia Farnham*

Quinoa (pronounced keen-wa) is a grain that comes from South America, high in the Andes Mountains, and has long been known as the mother grain. It's light and fluffy and will take on the flavors imparted by the recipe in which you are using it. In this salad the roasted garlic and nuttiness of the cauliflower, along with smoky notes of the cob bacon, bring this grain to new heights. *Serves 8*

1 cup quinoa (soak for 15 minutes and rinse in cool water)*

2 cups water

3 T olive oil

2 cloves garlic, crushed

4 green scallions, chopped

3 celery ribs, diced

1 C grape tomatoes, cut crosswise

½ large head each of cauliflower, white and purple, cut into1- inch florets

6 oz cob bacon, diced ¼-inch thick

¼ C extra-virgin olive oil

3 lemons juiced (about 5 Tablespoons)

¼ C chopped fresh flat-leaf parsley

1 tsp dried marjoram

4 oz diced Elk Mountain, a nutty flavored aged goat cheese (young Tarentaise or Comté will work)

Coarse salt and ground pepper to taste

In a large saucepan heat the olive oil. Add garlic and cook until it softens and the aroma mellows, 2–3 minutes.

Add celery and cauliflower, and cook until tender, adding a bit more oil as needed, 5–6 minutes. Toss in bacon, coat with olive oil and garlic, and cook 2 more minutes. Remove from heat and let cool for 10 minutes.

In your serving bowl combine prepared quinoa, scallion, tomatoes, olive oil, lemon juice, and herbs. Season with salt and pepper. Add vegetable mixture and combine well. Add the diced cheese last. Toss and serve.

*To prepare quinoa: Place quinoa and water in a 1½ quart saucepan and bring to a boil. Reduce to a simmer, cover, and cook until all the water is absorbed (about 15 minutes). Fluff gently with a fork and set aside to cool. The quinoa can be made ahead of time and refrigerated. *Makes 3 cups*

Try with . . .

Off the Vine: This vegetable-focused dish is terrific with a Sauvignon Blanc's lightly herbal, citrusy flavors. Try one from New Zealand, like the 2008 Babich Marlborough.

Appetite for Ale: The grain-driven beers have a floral aroma and malty finish that brings out the round, oaty flavors in this goat cheese. Try an English session beer like Organic Velvet ESB (Hopworks Urban Brewery, Portland, Oregon) or Rainbow Red Ale (Trout River Brewing Company, Lyndonville, Vermont).

❝ Think of all the stuff that's going on, you've got billions of organisms per milliliter—you've got so much life happening, so much complex stuff banging together . . . but it somehow follows a routine! **❞**

—JEFF JIRIK, Cheesemaker, Faribault Dairy

④
Coagulation and Drainage

MILK COAGULATION is the most exciting moment of chee-semaking. All the other steps are like watching grass grow. As a cheese-maker this moment should bring you some adrenaline. The main objec-tive of the coagulation step is to have an irreversible change of the milk from the liquid state to a semisolid state called a *gel* or *coagulum*. In order to have that phase change, you will need to use a coagulant.

Type of Coagulants

From animal sources	From microbial sources	From genetically modified microorganism	From plant sources
Rennet from calf, lamb, or kid	*Mucor miehei* (mold) *Mucor pusillus* (mold) *Endothia parasitica* (fungus)	*Escherichia coli* (bacteria) *Aspergillus awamori* (yeast)	Fig sap, Cardoon extract, Bromelain (pineapple)

As we can see in the table above, there are many different types of coagulant that can be used for cheesemaking. Let's take a closer look at the four different categories.

Coagulant from Animal Sources

The "rennet" used exclusively in Europe is extracted from the third stomach pocket of a ten- to thirty-day-old milk-fed ruminant. Calf rennet is the traditional coagulant that is the most often used for milk coagulation. It is fairly expensive and in short supply. This type of coagulant can be used for all the varieties of cheese.

Coagulant from Microbial Sources

Microbial coagulants have been widely used in the cheese industry with good success. However, lower cheese yields are obtained compared to use of animal coagulant. Coagulants from microbial sources are usually made from enzymes produced by *M. miehei* (mold). Aging of cheese made with microbial coagulant is sometimes quicker due to the stronger activity of the enzyme from the coagulant. Usually the proteins break down faster, which makes the cheese runnier. Coagulant from microbial sources can be used for the manufacturing process of soft cheeses but can be difficult to use with the lactic cheeses.

Genetically Engineered (GE) Coagulant

The GE coagulant is obtained from bacteria (*E. coli*) or yeast (*K. lactis*) that in general has been engineered to produce one of the enzymes in the animal coagulant called chymosin. This type of coagulant has excellent cheesemaking performance but can cause some marketing issues (GMO issue).

Coagulant from Plant Sources

Plant coagulants usually come from fig sap or cardoon. Despite its historical use, this type of coagulant doesn't render good results in comparison to the other types of coagulants. They tend to break down the proteins fairly aggressively, which lead to defects in the cheese, such as bitterness.

ABOVE: Preparation of coagulant from cardoon

The three most important parameters to observe during milk coagulation:

- The *time of flocculation*: This is the time between the addition of coagulant and the beginning of the flocculation.
- *The time of coagulation*: This is the time between the addition of the coagulant and the cutting time.
- The *firmness/resting time*: This is the time of coagulation minus time of flocculation.

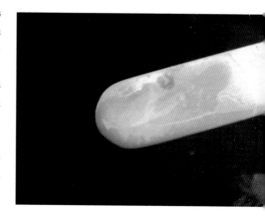

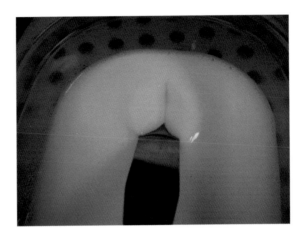

Rennet   flocculation

(Full) Coagulation time   Cutting

REACTION OCCURRING WHEN COAGULANT IS ADDED TO THE MILK:

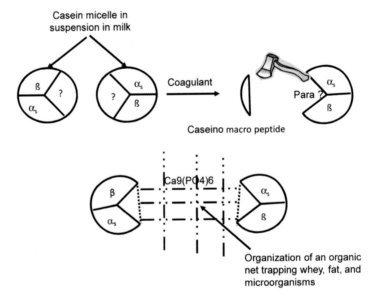

Casein micelle in
suspension in milk

Coagulant

Caseino macro peptide

Para ?

$Ca_9(PO_4)_6$

Organization of an organic
net trapping whey, fat, and
microorganisms

Time (min)

The first reaction occurring when the coagulant is added to the milk is that the casein micelles are being cut by the action of the coagulant's enzyme. The modified structures of the casein micelle begin to bond together. This is when we start to see flocculation happening. Finally, we let the coagulum rest for some more time until the gel has the desired resistance. At that time the bonds between the casein micelles become stronger. When you have the desired gel resistance (clean cut), this is time to cut the coagulum in small cubes.

A number of different variables, such as milk pH, milk microbial quality, and milk protein content will have a huge impact on the coagulation process during cheesemaking. In order to be consistent, cheesemakers use guidelines to estimate when the coagulum should be ready to cut.

Cheesemakers monitor the amount of time until the flocculation can be observed, then they multiply the flocculation time by a defined coefficient in order to estimate when the coagulum is ready to cut. The coefficient is based on the family the cheese is classified in.

Cheese family	Multiplier coefficient
Soft cheese	2
Semihard cheese	1
Hard cheese	0.5–0.8

Application

If you are trying to make a soft cheese and you observe that it takes 10 minutes for the milk to flocculate, you will need to let the coagulum rest for another 20 minutes (2 x10 min). The total coagulation time with the addition of the coagulant and the cutting time should be approximately 30 minutes (20 minutes for the resting time and 10 minutes for the flocculation time).

The most important thing is to check for a clean cut.

How to properly measure and calculate the amount of coagulant *for more than 20 gallons of milk*

First, you need to calculate the amount of coagulant needed for the volume of milk that you are using.

If you are using 28 gallons of milk, and are following the cheese-making procedure for a soft bloomy-rind cheese (described in the cheese make chapter), you would add 20ml of animal coagulant for 100L (26.45 gallons) of milk.

The first thing that you need to calculate is how much coagulant you need to use for your 28 gallons of milk.

Second, figure out how many milliliters of coagulant you will need based on the volume of milk that you have.

Example: If we have 28 gallons of milk in the vat, how much coagulant are you going to need?

20 ml	26.45 gallons of milk
? ml	28 gallons of milk in our cheese vat

? ml = (20 * 28) / 26.45

? ml = 21 ml

With 28 gallons of milk in the cheese vat, you will need to use 21ml of coagulant.

How to properly measure and calculate the amount of coagulant *for less than 20 gallons of milk:*

It is a little difficult to properly measure the amount of coagulant for a small amount of milk. Most cheesemaking resources recommend the use of "drops," which is not accurate. Therefore, you will need to use some tricks in order to be more accurate.

First, you need to calculate the amount of coagulant needed for the volume of milk that you are using.

If you are using 5 gallons of milk and are following the cheesemaking procedure for a fresh unripened goat milk cheese (described in the cheese make chapter) you would add 5 ml of animal coagulant for 100L (26.45 gallons) of milk.

The first thing that you will need to calculate is how much coagulant you will need to use for your 5 gallons of milk.

Second, figure out how many milliliters of coagulant you will need based on the volume of milk that you have.

Example: If we have 5 gallons of milk in the vat, how much coagulant are you going to need?

5 ml   26.45 gallons of milk

? ml   3 gallons of milk in our cheese vat

? ml = (5 * 3) / 26.45

? ml = 0.57 ml

With 3 gallons of milk in the cheese vat you will need to use 0.57ml of coagulant, which is a very small amount to measure.

Third, in order to measure an extremely small amount of coagulant, you will need to make a dilution.

Mix 1ml of coagulant   20ml of cold water

(Make sure the water is not chlorinated)

Once we have mixed the coagulant well, we need to calculate how much of the solution we need to measure for cheesemaking.

Example: If we have 1ml of coagulant mixed with 20ml of cold water, how much of the diluted coagulant we are going to need for the 3 gallons of milk in the vat?

1 ml of coagulant   20ml of cold water

In theory, we need 0.57ml of coagulant   ?ml of diluted coagulant

? ml of diluted coagulant = (0.57 * 20) / 1

? ml = 11.5 ml

With 3 gallons of milk in our cheese vat we will need to use 11.5ml of diluted coagulant.

Equipment Needed

Equipment	Description	URL
Measuring cylinder	Thermo Scientific Nalgene graduated polymethylpentene cylinder, 25 mL	www.coleparmer.com
Measuring cylinder	Measuring cylinder, 10 mL (0.1ml increments)	www.angelgilding.com

Curd Drainage

Drainage of the cheese curd is one of the most critical steps of cheesemaking. There are different techniques that can be employed in order to remove a certain amount of moisture from the cheese curds based on the type of cheese that you are making.

First drainage technique: cutting the coagulum (gel)

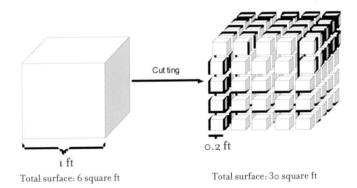

Cutting

1 ft

Total surface: 6 square ft

0.2 ft

Total surface: 30 square ft

Curd size (cm)	Curd volume (cm³)	For 0.1m³ (100L/26.45gallons) of gel	
		Number of curds	Surface area (m²)
2 x 2 x 2	8	12,500	30
1.5 x 1.5 x 1.5	3.375	29,600	40
1 x 1 x 1	1	100,000	60
0.75 x 0.75 x 0.75	0.42	237,000	80

(Continued)

RIGHT: Perdido Cheese

I grew my own, there was such an improvement in flavor and such a difference in the quality of cheese."

Not only do they grow their own food, but they glue, plumb, mow, and fix anything and everything that they can by themselves. "We like to do everything from scratch."

Alyce is a member of the Southern Cheesemakers' Guild, the American Cheese Society, and the Raw Milk Cheesemakers' Association. While she has won many national awards, Alyce is not about the competition. "I compete as a point of interest rather than because I am compelled."

Pasta with Spring Peas, Asparagus, Pancetta, and Asiago

This pasta dish is an excellent way to use the early spring vegetables that are just starting to show up at the farmers' market. Locally grown, fresh asparagus and peas couldn't be more tender and sweet in this dish, and shelling the peas, well, it's just relaxing. The addition of the smoky pancetta and pungent Italian-style cheese seasoned with whole peppercorns rounds out this surprisingly easy springtime recipe. *Serves 4 main or 6 small plates*

12 oz orecchiette or other pasta

3 oz pancetta (Italian bacon), chopped, or try prosciutto

1¼ lbs asparagus, trimmed, cut on diagonal into 1-inch pieces

2 C shelled fresh green peas, blanched 1 minute in boiling water, drained

6 green scallions, thinly sliced

3 garlic cloves, pressed

½ C finely grated Pepato Asiago (Sweet Home Farm) plus additional for serving (grated Parmesan works well)

½ C heavy cream

3 T extra-virgin olive oil

3 T fresh lemon juice

1 T finely grated lemon peel

¼ C chopped fresh Italian parsley, divided

¼ C thinly sliced fresh basil, divided

Coarse salt and ground black pepper

Cook pasta in pot of boiling salted water until just tender.

Drain, reserve ½ cup pasta cooking liquid. Return pasta to pot.

Meanwhile, cook pancetta in large nonstick skillet over medium heat until crisp.

Using slotted spoon, transfer pancetta to paper towels and drain. Reserve 1 teaspoon of the drippings in the skillet.

Add asparagus to drippings; sauté 3 minutes.

Add peas, scallions and garlic; sauté until vegetables are just tender, about 3 more minutes. Remove from heat.

To the pasta, add vegetable mixture, ¼ cup pasta cooking liquid, ½ cup Pepato Asiago, cream, olive oil, lemon juice, lemon peel, half of parsley, and half of basil.

Toss, continue to add more cooking liquid by tablespoonfuls if needed, creating a loose creamy sauce. Season with salt and freshly ground pepper. Transfer to large bowl. Sprinkle pancetta, remaining parsley, and basil over top. Serve, offering additional grated Pepato Asiago or Parmesan cheese.

Try with . . .

Off the Vine: Pinot noir is typically a lighter-bodied, fruit-forward red wine that pairs well with the Asiago and pancetta in this dish. Its cherries, plums, and notable earthy, something peppery notes combine for perfection. Try Coppola Diamond Series pinot noir. A Chardonnay is a well-rounded white for this dish. 2007 Clos du Bois Chardonnay Reserve Russian River Valley (easy to find) has lush aromas of pears, toasty oak, and sweet spice, complementing the sweetness of the peas and contrasting with the pepper of the cheese.

Appetite for Ales: Belgian Dubbels, a rich malty beer with some spice. German Rauchbier's aroma is strong and smoky, and its flavor is clean and powerful yet delicate, not overwhelming. Both pair well with the smoky pancetta and creamy sauce.

" It is wonderful feeling a part of something [cheesemaking] that has been here a long, long time before you were here . . . **"**

—JULY SCHAD, Capriole Farm

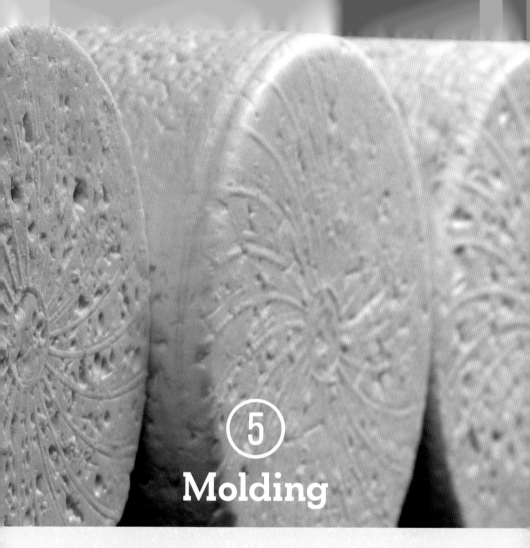

⑤
Molding

THE MAIN GOAL of molding the cheese curds is to remove the cheese curds from the whey and to shape the cheese. There are currently three different molding techniques that allow you to obtain different varieties of cheese texture.

Blind cheeses with no mechanical holes

It is very typical to not want any mechanical holes in cheeses such as Gouda, Beaufort, Comté, Morbier, and Raclette.

In order to achieve that result, most small cheesemakers prepress (a very light pressure) the cheese curds under the whey for a few minutes. This allows for a nice fusion of curds, producing a nice smooth texture without the formation of holes. Sometimes you can see pinholes appear in the cheese paste. The small holes formed are due to the gas production

ABOVE: Small holes formed are due to gas production; they are fine in this type of cheese.

of some heterofermentative bacteria. They are fine in these types of cheese.

Cheeses with mechanical holes

Some types of cheese, such as Roquefort, Fourme d'Ambert, and Bleu d'Auvergne, are going to require the formation of a lot of mechanical holes. These mechanical holes are going to trap some air that will later be used for the development of blue molds in the cheese.

The formation of mechanical holes is obtained by draining all the whey out of the cheese vat followed by dry stirring to the cheese curds. Once the cheese curds are exposed to the air, we are drying the peripheries of the curds, which will lead to a lack of cohesion between the curds resulting in the formation of mechanical holes.

BELOW: Note the mechanical holes here.

LEFT: Prepressing table to press the cheese curds under whey.

Cheeses with layers in the body

These cheeses include the aged lactic goat cheeses, such as Crottin de Chavignol and Valencay. When you look at the cheese texture after cutting a wedge it looks very smooth. However, if you try to break down the cheese texture between your fingers, you will quickly realize that the texture is peeling off in layers. It is very typical in the aged (once the cheese paste is a little bit dryer) lactic cheeses that are ladled. When the cheesemaker is ladling the gel into the molds, it creates a weak point in the cheese that will cause the lactic aged cheese to break up by layers.

The first goat that Judy Schad owned was dreadful. "The goat was dreadful, and her milk was dreadful," recalls Judy, owner and head cheesemaker of Indiana's only commercial goat dairy, Capriole Farm. "I

BELOW: Dry stirring the cheese curd.

don't know why we ever got another one." But she and her husband did get another. In fact, they got many a goat more and now manage a herd of 500. It is thanks to these goats that Capriole's delicious, award-winning cheeses can be enjoyed by the masses.

Judy's grandparents gave her the cooking and gardening bug and originally inspired her to buy a farm of her own. In 1976 she and her husband Larry moved their family from the city out to an 80-acre farmstead in Greenville in search of a more natural and sustainable lifestyle. Ironically, when researching the title for the farm, they discovered that Larry's great-great grandfather had owned it during the 1870s, and they felt as though they had truly come home. "It was the 1970s and everyone was into the "back to the land" thing. We were nuts." But since then, Judy has proven that there was a method to her madness.

She started making fresh goat cheese in the kitchen of her farmhouse with nothing but a sink and her dreadful goat's milk to facilitate the process. It didn't take long for her to realize that this was something

LEFT: Judy and Little One.

ABOVE: Piper's Pyramid, fresh Chèvre sprinkled with paprika.

she really enjoyed. She began refining her cheesemaking skills by taking classes and working with other artisan cheesemakers. She soon began selling her goat cheeses under the name Capriole, aptly titled, as a *capriole* is a happy little dance goats do by executing a little leap and twirl with all four feet leaving the ground. In 1990, she and her husband built a cheese plant right on the farm.

"We knew that we would never be able to compete in the market with the volume of cheese we produced, so we had to make our cheese distinctive." Judy began working with raw milk and French-inspired molds to help differentiate her cheeses. "The combination of milk and mold we use makes our cheeses very different." Instead of a thick, leathery mold, Capriole's cheese dons a thin, light, wrinkly surface.

Then, there's the milk. "We cannot do what we do without the animals. If there came a day when we could no longer take care of them, then that would be the end the cheesemaking business for us." Raised in rotating woodland paddocks and fed on homegrown hay, Capriole's goats are born on the farm and live out their lives there. Since it is a closed herd, pedigrees can be traced back at least 20 generations for most of the animals. Yes, each and every one of the goats is named. "We manage our goat herd like princesses. It's like a city girl with her dogs."

Princesses indeed; in fact at one point the entire herd bowed to Judy as their queen, making getting back to the house quite a trick. You see, in the wild goats are led by a queen. They usually choose one or two old girls to follow, and wherever the queen goes, they go. Judy became their adopted queen. "I would go for walks in the woods and all the goats would follow. I would have to hide behind trees to escape them."

Besides being the only commercial goat farm in Indiana, Capriole also differentiates itself by milking their goats year-round. Using lights to trick the goats, they are able to breed them for all 12 months of the year, rather than the usual May to October. "When we first started out there were no farmers' markets, and we needed to find a national market. We had no choice but to go year-round."

These days, Judy still works year-round and spends five or six hours a day in the cheese plant. With the help of ten employees split between the farm and cheesemaking, she is able to produce 60,000 pounds of cheese per year, a far cry from the small kitchen-made batches of fresh goat cheese that got her started more than two decades ago. "After all these years, I still love ladling a vat of cheese. I find it very spiritual. The

ABOVE: Capriole's aged, raw milk Cheese, named Julianna

smell, the feelings, the flavors. It's very repetitive, and it's a very beautiful thing."

Capriole's cheeses come in many different shapes, sizes, and varieties, and, not unlike the goats, are all given special names. "We were encouraged to come up with names that reflected who we are and where we came from—Wabash Cannonball, O'Banon, Old Kentucky Tomme, and Mont St. Francis all have very personal connections." You can find these cheeses as well as the many others at local farmers' markets, grocers, and cheese shops, and in restaurants. The cheeses are also distributed nationally.

Capriole has made quite a name for itself over the past twenty-three years, winning Best of Show at the American Cheese Society and being sold all across the country. "It is wonderful feeling a part of something that has been here a long, long time before you were here and hopefully for a long, long time after you are gone."

Capriole, Inc.

Owner and cheesemaker: Judy Schad
Greenville, Indiana
E-mail: caprioleinc@aol.com
Website: www.capriolegoatcheese.com

Roasted Beet Salad with Pears, Chèvre, and Pecans

Luscious red beets are among the delights of a late summer garden. Roasted and tossed with creamy goat cheese and toasted nuts, their vibrant color and meaty goodness make this dish a delicious addition to any late summer feast. *Serves 12*

½ C pecan halves, toasted

4 bunches of small beets (16–18) or 8–10 larger beets

2 ripe pears

1 T cider vinegar

2 T balsamic vinegar

3 T olive oil (use the good stuff)

4 oz fresh goat cheese, crumbled (Chèvre logs or rounds from Capriole Farm)

2 freshly chopped parsley, plus a few sprigs for garnish

1 T fresh thyme (tiny leaves pull from stem)

Coarse salt and fresh ground pepper to taste

Preheat oven to 350°F.

Place pecans on a baking sheet and toast until fragrant, about 6 minutes. Watch closely. Transfer to a bowl to cool.

Trim greens and long roots off the beets, cut in half, and place face-down in a baking dish (may need two dishes), sprinkle with a bit of salt, and add a dash of water to pan. Cover with aluminum foil, place in oven, roast until tender, 50–60 minutes, depending on the size of the beets.

Once out of the oven and cool, the skins will come off easily with a dry paper towel. (Beets can be roasted a day or two ahead.)

Cut beets and pears into slices or wedges and place in the serving bowl. Add the pecans.

Whisk the vinegars and olive oil together and add the salt and pepper, and drizzle over the beets toss to coat.

Close to service add the goat cheese, parsley, and salt and pepper to taste. Garnish with more parsley or other herbs from the garden.

Try with . . .

Off the Vine: This is a side dish, I know, but the magical combination of the tart goat cheese, sweetness of the beets, and toasted goodness of the nuts is just crying for a pinot noir from the Northern Pacific. Try a Special reserve pinot noir from either Rex Hill or Argyle Vineyards, Willamette Valley.

Appetite for Ale: Pair with a medium-bodied and well-hopped IPA with a dry and fruity finish. Try Commodore Perry IPA (Great Lakes Brewing Company).

French Presses for Beaufort cheese

" We do not use any chemicals in the pastures, so there are no health risks with the raw milk in that way, and we don't do anything fancy with our cheeses, but we use a high-quality raw milk. Raw milk makes a better cheese. **"**

—NEIL URIE, Bonnieview Farm

Pressing

THE MAIN GOAL of pressing is to give shape to the cheese (round or rectangular) and more important to remove the whey from between the cheese curds. Most cheeses and all hard cheeses will need to be pressed in order to remove even more moisture out of the cheese matrix.

TARGET PRESSURES FOR DIFFERENT VARIETIES OF CHEESE

Cheese type	Pressure in gram per square centimeter	Pressure in pound per square inch
Reblochon-type cheese	15	0.21
Gouda cheese for nonmicroperforated form	200	2.84
Hard cooked cheese for nonmicroperforated form	200–300	2.84–4.26
Cheddar cheese for nonmicroperforated form	800	11.35

Hint: If you have molds with very few holes, you may have to increase the amount of pressure on the form slightly.

How to calculate the amount of weight to put on the mold if you don't have any cheese press:

As it is indicated above the amount of pressure needed on the cheese is based on the surface area of the cheese. If your cheese is round you can calculate the surface area with the following equation:

(3.14 x diameter of your form x diameter of your form) / 4

Example: if you have a round mold of 10 cm diameter and you are trying to make a Gouda cheese, you will need to put 15,700g of pressure on the form.

(3.14 x 10 x 10) / 4 = 314 square centimeter

314 x 200 = 15,700g or 15.7 kg or 34.54 lbs.

How to calculate the amount of pressure to read on pressure gauge:

Example: you have a cheese of a diameter of 140mm, and you have a cheese press that has a piston shaft diameter of 65mm. You will need to apply 120g/cm². How can you calculate which pressure should read on your cheese press?

1/ Convert the pressure needed on the cheese to the international unit: Pascal (Pa).

120 x 100 = 12,000 Pa

2/ Calculate the Force in Newton (N) that needs to be applied to the cheese.

=Pressure in Pa on the cheese x Surface area of the cheese = 12,000 x (~3.14 (π) x 0.070 x 0.070 = 185N

3/ Divide the Force (N) on the cheese by the surface area of the piston shaft of the cheese press.

= 185/(~3.14 (π) x 0.0325 x 0.0325) = 55,751 Pa = 0.5 Bar

How do you press a cheese wheel?

The best way to press a wheel is to increase the pressure two or three times during the pressing step. If you press too hard at the very beginning, a rind will form really quickly, and the cheese won't drain properly.

ABOVE: Thomasville Tomme-Sweet Grass Dairy.

A city boy at heart, Jeremy Little never imagined that one day he would find himself the owner of a goat dairy in a small Southern town making artisan cheese for a living. At the age of thirty-three, Jeremy lives with his wife, Jessica, and four sons at Sweet Grass Dairy, a 140-acre goat farm in Thomasville, Georgia. It is here that this sworn urbanite turned country-lover makes award-winning goat's- and cow's-milk cheeses.

Although farming and cheesemaking weren't on his radar as a young college graduate in Tallahassee, Florida, Jeremy always had an inclination toward a career in the food world. "I wanted to own a restaurant; I always cooked meals for my roommates, had cookbooks, and wanted to go to culinary school." It wasn't until 2002, however, when Jeremy's in-laws, Al and Desiree Wehner, the original owners of Sweet Grass, invited him down to stay on the farm, that Jeremy's life changed. "The farming aspect of life was so foreign to me. They were in such a small town, and I was a city boy. My wife and I would always go down to the farm for a few days and then leave."

This time was different. Jeremy jumped in with both feet and wore whatever hat was needed on the farm. "I thought I knew about food until I came down here. I really had no clue what food was. I always thought that as long as I went to the produce section of the grocery store that I knew where my food came from. Being on the farm, I really saw what it was about."

It was during this period that he started helping his mother-in-law make cheese. "I started making cheese kind of trial by fire. My mother-in-law would tell me to throw in the rennet one day so I would do that, or follow the recipe the next day and I would do that." By 2004 Jeremy was Sweet Grass's cheesemaker. When Desiree and Al were ready to sell Sweet Grass in 2005, Jeremy and Jessica were there to take it over, he as the cheesemaker and she as the marketing guru.

"It took us a year after buying it to realize that the farm was really ours and that we could do what we wanted with it. What is our legacy? We wanted to take what my mother-in-law got started and make it bigger."

Jeremy and Jessica continued the practice of a sustainable grass-based system for their 140 resident goats started by Al and Desiree. Twelve five- to ten-acre pastures on the farm allow for the goats to be rotationally grazed, offering the most lush grass and forage available on the farm. Each pasture has a wooded area where the goats can browse, as they prefer to do. Since Sweet Grass Dairy doesn't have any barns on their property, the goats are able to use the trees as protection from the weather, if needed. Most important, the animals live their entire lives outside in green pastures, leaving them healthy, happy, and able to produce rich and delicious milk. Jeremy makes 10,000–20,000 pounds of goat's milk cheese each year, with names like Kelle's Blue, Holly Springs, Dante, and Lumiere.

In addition to the goat's-milk cheese, Jeremy also makes 75,000 pounds of cow's-milk cheese per year using milk from Jersey cows at his father-in-law's Green Hill Dairy. Like the goats at Sweet Grass, the cows are rotationally grazed rather than raised by the more conventional method of confinement barns on concrete. They have a handful of cheeses made from a goat's and cow's milk mix as well, including their Crossroads Blue and Hopeful Tomme.

Over the years, Sweet Grass has won more than twenty national awards for its cheeses, including a bronze medal for their Asher Blue at the World Cheese Awards, as well as first place two years in a row in 2007 and 2008 from the American Cheese Society for its Green Hill, a pasteurized, soft-ripened cow's milk cheese.

Obviously, the folks at Sweet Grass have great success with their cheese, but their accomplishments do not stop there. In fact, they have put in a great deal of effort to give back and help improve quality of life in their community, offering school tours and a summer camp to teach children about the importance of knowing where their food comes from. "We are a little sneaky that way, going through the kids. We hope they will bring what they learn home to the parents."

Sweet Grass cheeses can be found all across the country, from California to Connecticut, in restaurants and retail shops. "We sell cheeses all over the place with people who do business the way we do. We work with people who make a difference in the marketplace and have a mutual respect for us and others."

Although it took a little maneuvering to get Jeremy to where he is today, his success with Sweet Grass Dairy and his cheeses have proven that he is finally on the right track. "I love the challenge. I'm really excited about where we are going. I love pushing the limit about how much further we can go."

Sautéed Pears with Honey and Blue Cheese

This dessert is especially wonderful when Bosc pears are in season, but any local pears will do. Although the pear takes center stage here, the Blue cheese is what will set this dessert apart from other summer delights. The convergence of sweet honey and almost brown butter create a sauce that is caramelly and rich with nutty flavors. Then voilà! Kelle's Blue cheese is crumbled on top to bring down the curtain on this savory, salty goodness. Your just dessert! *Serves 6*

¼ C unsalted butter

3 Bosc or Anjou pears, firm but ripe (halved lengthwise, and cored)

3½ T mild honey (such as clover, local if possible)

1–2 tsp apple cider or port wine

4 oz Kelle's Blue cheese (Sweet Grass Dairy) or your local blue

3 T pine nuts

6 Sprigs of fresh mint

Pinch of coarse salt

Cook unsalted butter in large nonstick pan over medium-high heat until it begins to brown.

Place the pear halves cut side down, into the skillet. Drizzle with honey and swirl pan to blend butter and honey into mixture.

Reduce heat to medium, cover, and let cook until pears are tender, swirling the pan occasionally, about 14 minutes. Add a little cider to pears if caramel sauce turns thick before pears are tender.

Transfer pears, cut side up, to serving plate and let cool.

Return pan with sauce to cook over medium-high heat; add pine nuts to skillet and sprinkle with salt. Cook until caramel sauce is bubbling and nuts are roasted—about 2 minutes.

Spoon over pears, crumble Blue cheese on top, add fresh mint to plate, and serve.

Try with . . .

Off the Vine: A dessert wine or late harvest wine with notes of, what else . . . pear and honey combination! Try JC Cellars Ripkin Vineyard Late Harvest Viognier (Kirkland Ranch Winery) or Agape Late Harvest (Napa Valley, California).

Appetite for Ale: Indian Pale Ale; like Smuttynose IPA (Smuttynose Brewing Company, Portsmouth, New Hampshire).

Sweet Grass Dairy

Owners: Jeremy & Jessica Little
Cheesemaker: Jeremy Little
Thomasville, Georgia
E-mail: info@sweetgrassdairy.com
Website: www.sweetgrassdairy.com

" We will only use milk from optimum pastures when the cows can fill up and lay down in the lush grass. In the interest of consistency, we select the days to make cheese. The cheese intensifies and becomes more complex at its peak. The peak is different for each cheese. **"**

— **MIKE GINGRICH, Uplands Cheese Company**

Students dry salting by hand on Blue cheese.

⑦

Salting: Brining vs. Dry Salting

THE MAIN GOAL of the salting step is to regulate the micro-biological and enzymatic activities of the cheese during the aging process. Salting the cheese will enhance the flavor and prolong the shelf life of the cheese. Different cheese varieties will require different amounts of salt, different salting techniques, and different duration of exposure to the salt.

TARGET PRESSURE FOR DIFFERENT VARIETIES OF CHEESE

Cheese type	Minimum salt content (%)	Maximum salt content (%)
Swiss cheese	0.4	0.6
Tomme de Savoie	1.4	2.0
Reblochon cheese	1.3	1.5
Camembert cheese	1.2	1.7
Roquefort	3	3.6

Dry salting vs. brine salting:

Dry salting and brine salting are the two major techniques for salting cheese. Brine salting requires mixing water and salt. Often cheesemakers will use a saturated brine solution, which is easier to maintain because you just have to be sure that you always have some residual salt in the bottom of the brine tank after stirring. Usually you mix about 357g of salt/liter (2.97 lbs of salt/gallon) of water to obtain a saturated brine solution at 10°C/50°F. The pH of the brine is adjusted to the pH of the cheese when a new brine is being made. This prevents a mineral shift from the cheese matrix to the brine. Any type of acid can be used to standardize the pH of the brine solution. Acetic acid (vinegar) works great. The dryer and the more mineralized and/or the bigger the cheese, the longer you will have to brine the cheese. As a rule of thumb, you would usually brine a Gouda cheese 3–3.5H /lbs of cheese.

The other technique used to salt cheese is dry salting. It is mainly used by small dairy operations and homestead cheesemakers because of the ease of application. If you simply want to salt the cheese use regular fine salt. If you are trying to salt the cheese to cause some mechanical action, rubbing with some coarse salt will work.

How to measure the amount of salt needed for dry salting?

Example: How to salt a Camembert cheese.

Take the average weight of your cheese and add 1.9 percent of salt by weight. If your Camembert weighs 350g, add 6.65g of salt (350 x 1.9)/100 =6.65) on each cheese. If you have ten cheeses, you will need a total of 66.5g of salt. Take half of it (33.25g) and salt your cheese with a

RIGHT: Rubbing coarse salt during Blue cheese cheesemaking.

saltshaker. An hour or two later, flip the cheese and salt the other side. During the salting step, you will lose a little bit of salt. This why we have been measuring 1.9 percent salt in order to achieve a final salt intake between 1.5 and 1.7 percent

The aptly named Uplands Cheese Company hangs its hat among the rolling hills and valleys of the Upland Region of Southern Wisconsin. Run by cheesemaker Mike Gingrich, Uplands is internationally known for its one and only cheese, Pleasant Ridge Reserve, created with the milk from 200 pasture-fed Wisconsin cows. When Mike first began making cheese, he was told by many of his Wisconsin counterparts that his pasture milk would not taste any different than their commercial milk. He forged ahead anyway and now has a uniquely flavored, award-winning cheese to show for it.

Mike was introduced to dairy farming as a young child, spending summers with his maternal grandparents on their dairy farm. However, it wasn't until his mid-thirties, after a stint in an office, that he decided to make farming his full-time job. "My mother's family were all dairy farmers, and I admired the sort of life they were able to live. My children were getting older, and I wanted them to have the experience of growing up on a farm because I loved the time I spent on my grandparents' farm—my children hated it, by the way."

After owning his own small dairy farm for ten years, Mike and his wife decided to partner with another Couple to purchase Grass Dairy, Inc, a 300-acre cow dairy that boasts twenty ridgetop pastures for their cows to graze. "We bought the larger farm strictly for the rotational grazing. We manicure our pastures to ensure optimum grazing." Each day the cows are brought to a different pasture and given the best grasses, herbs, and wildflowers to eat.

Mike knew that the milk they were producing had unique flavor properties due to the cows' forage, but any uniqueness was being diluted with milks from conventional dairy farms when it was sold. "Our milk was getting mixed in with everyone else's milk. In order to save the uniqueness, we decided to make cheese." And thus, Uplands Cheese and Pleasant Ridge Reserve were born.

An original, handcrafted, raw-milk cheese reminiscent of the French Gruyère–style cheeses, Pleasant Ridge Reserve, named for the area of southwest Wisconsin from whence it hails, was first made in 1999 at the University of Wisconsin and then aged in Mike's basement. As the process became more refined, in 2000 Uplands moved its cheesemaking to a local cheese factory and paid them to use their equipment, making 6,000 pounds of cheese that year. This was the first time they were able to sell their product to customers. Finally, in 2004, after making cheese off-site for four years, Mike built a cheese house of his own not eighty yards from the barn. "As our volume grew the inefficiencies of doing everything off-site was too time consuming and the larger market we were serving could justify the cost of building an on-farm plant."

Nowadays, the fresh milk makes its way from the milk house through a pipeline laid underneath his driveway to the cheese house twice daily. With the help of one other full-time cheesemaker and eight part-timers, Mike works to make 100,000 pounds of cheese from May to October, a far cry from the smaller batches made back at the University.

The amount of cheese they produce is quite a feat, as they don't make cheese every day during their growing season, which averages around 170 days. Instead, they only make cheese 125–140 days depending on the year. "We will only use milk from optimum pastures when the cows can fill up and lay down in the lush grass. In the interest of consistency, we select the days to make cheese."

Once the cheese is made, it is aged for four months before it is sold. Mike suggests trying the cheese at different ages, as it may taste different. "The cheese intensifies and becomes more complex at its peak. The peak is different for each cheese." However, Pleasant Ridge has won all of its national awards when the cheeses have aged somewhere between eight and ten months.

Their practices have proved extremely successful. They won the American Cheese Society's Best of Show the first year they entered in 2001. "Winning this award really validated all our assumptions. There really was a connection between the cows' diet and the flavors in the cheese." They won Best of Show again in 2005 and have added many national competition awards, including U.S. Champion at the 2003 U.S. Championship Cheese Contest, making Pleasant Ridge Reserve the only cheese to win both national awards.

Pleasant Ridge Reserve is distributed nationally and sold direct to customers. It has also been requested overseas in London.

Three-Cheese Fondue

The pairing of good friends and good cheese comes together at its best with this quintessential Swiss dish, fondue. The combination of cheese and wine is delicious and friendly. Don't heat the cheese beyond its melting point; slow and low works best. *Serves 8 to 10*

1 clove garlic, halved crosswise

1½ C dry white wine

8 oz Pleasant Ridge Reserve cheese, grated (3 cups)

8 oz Tarentaise cheese, grated (1½ cups)

4 oz Raclette cheese, grated (3 cups)

2 T freshly squeezed Meyer lemon juice

2 T cornstarch

Freshly grated nutmeg (when you start to smell it, that's enough)

Freshly ground white pepper

1 loaf toasted rustic bread, cut into 1-inch cubes

Assorted fresh or steamed vegetables, such as cauliflower, broccoli, and red bell pepper.

Try button mushrooms or roasted new potatoes. For a meatier fondue experience try summer sausage, roast pork, or tofu cut into bite-size pieces.

Rub inside of fondue pot with garlic; discard garlic.

Pour cider or wine into pot, and place over medium-low heat. When liquid starts to bubble, start adding cheeses by the handful, stirring until melted and combined.

Whisk together lemon juice and cornstarch in a small bowl until cornstarch dissolves; stir into cheese mixture. Continue stirring until mixture is smooth and bubbling slightly, about 5 minutes.
Season with nutmeg and pepper.
Transfer fondue pot to table, and keep warm over the fondue-pot flame. Serve with bread and veggies and charcuterie.

Try with . . .

Off the Vine: Sparkling wine: Prosecco, Cremant, or a Viognier will enhance flavor and add carbonation to help cleanse the palate of this thick delicious cheese fondue. Try either of these well-priced, delicious wines, Zardetto Prosecco Conegliano or La Marca Prosecco.

Appetite for Ale: Amber brown ales—this beer style will have roasted, nutty notes complementing the cooked cheese flavors in the dish. Try a Saint Rogue Red (Rouge Ales, Newport, Oregon) or Copper Ale (Otter Creek Brewing Company, Middlebury, Vermont).

Uplands Cheese Company
· ·

Owners & Cheesemakers: Mike and Carol Gingrich
Dodgeville, Wisconsin
E-mail: contact@uplandscheese.com
Website: www.uplandscheese.com

"Twenty-six years ago goat cheese and crème fraiche on the American table were but a fantasy. Fortunately we renounced the distracting nay-saying and adversity and held tight to the basic premise that if we believed in the cheeses that we loved to make and eat every day, nurtured our business and our customers, eventually the market would grow and support us."

—ALLISON HOOPER, Vermont Butter and Cheese Creamery

Aging

THE MAIN GOAL of aging cheese is to manage the different interactions between the different microorganisms used during the cheesemaking process. After being a cheesemaker for many years you will become an *affineur*. The role of an *affineur* is to make sure that the different flora that evolve in a cheese are growing well at the right rate.

Aging as a general process:

No matter what type of cheese we are making, the aging process will have the same basics steps. The main difference is the intensity of those steps, which will change according to the cheese type we are trying to age.

The first step of the aging process is the dehydration of the cheese. Most cheeses will lose some weight (moisture) by going through a dry-

LEFT: Cheese is placed on wooden shelves for aging and tagged with date and make.

PHOTO CREDIT: *Sara Forest*

ing room. It is not always necessary to send the cheese through a drying room. The drying room is a room that is usually warm (13–17°C/55–63°F) with a low relative humidity (75–85 percent). Some cheeses can lose a lot of weight going through that step. For example lactic goat cheeses can lose up to 30 percent of their weight in three to four days in the drying room. The main objective of the drying room is to remove any excess moisture in and/or on the cheese, which will help in rind development.

The second step that will occur is the deacidification process (unless you are making a rindless cheese such as a Cheddar, Gouda, etc). The deacidification process occurs at the same time as the dehydration step. The warm atmosphere in the drying room provides the yeast with a suitable environment for their development. Most of the time, the yeast have been added to the milk with the starter culture. Take a look at the diagram given for the Camembert cheese manufacturing process. We use some KL 71 (*Kluyveromyces lactis*), which is a yeast that will deacidify the cheese and will help to promote the development of other molds. Once the cheese surface has deacidified enough, other molds like *Penicillium camemberti* or bacteria like *Brevibacterium linens* will develop on the surface on the cheeses. Often, the microorganisms developing on the cheese surface have strong proteolytic and lipolytic activity. If we take the example of the *P. camemberti*, we realize that this mold has both proteolytic and lipolytic activity. If we look at a Camembert cheese, we see

that sometimes the cheese paste is a little runny underneath the rind due to too much proteolytic activity of the mold. The lipolytic activity will be responsible for most of the flavor and aroma development of the cheese.

Example of various aging cycles for different cheese families

CAMEMBERT CHEESE (BLOOMY-RIND CHEESE)

For Camembert cheese, you will look for the development of a succession of flora on the surface of the cheese. First, you will have the development of the yeast (KL 71), then when the pH increases a little bit, you will see the appearance of a very thin and sparse layer of white growth; this is *G. candidum* (usually four to five days during the aging process). Finally we will see the growth of *P. camemberti*, which will completely cover the cheese with a dense white mold.

LEFT:
Camembert round.

	If the cheese is brined	Aging	Wrap
Condition	Remove excess moisture in a drying room at 14–15°C/57–59°F with a relative humidity of 85% for approx. 24H	Age the cheese at 12–13°C/54–55°F with a relative humidity of 92–95%	Cool off the cheese at 4°C/39°F for about 24H before wrapping the cheese to avoid condensation
Aging care	Turn the cheese daily	Turn the cheese daily	Use a multiplex paper so the mold can breathe
Time	Immediately after the cheese is being salted	Age the cheese for 10 to 15 days	Wrap the cheese when the mold has fully covered the cheese

REBLOCHON-TYPE CHEESE (MIXED-RIND CHEESE—BETWEEN A SMEAR-RIND CHEESE AND A BLOOMY-RIND CHEESE)

For Reblochon-type cheese, you will also look for the development of a succession of flora on the surface of the cheese. First, you will have the development of the yeast (*Debaryomyces hansenii* and *Geotrichum candidum*, which are included in the PLA cocktail from Danisco). Then, when the yeast start to develop, the surface of the cheese will become really greasy, and the pH on the surface will increase. Then the orange *Brevibacterium linens* and the *Arthrobacter nicotianae* will start to develop.

LEFT:
Reblochon cheese.

	Warm room	Aging	Wrap
Condition	Boost the yeast growth by placing the cheese at 18°C/64°F with a relative humidity of 95–100% for approx. 4 to 8 days	Age the cheese at 13°C/55°F with a relative humidity of 90–94%	Cool the cheese at 4°C/39°F for about 24H before wrapping the cheese to avoid condensation
Aging care	Turn the cheese daily and wash the cheese with a smearing solution made of water and 6% salt (w/w) once before going to the aging room on the fourth day	Wash the cheese with a smearing solution (water + 6% salt (w/w) + 2 Dose of PLA). Rehydrate the solution 24H before its use. Wash the cheese every day at the beginning and space out the washing steps as the cheese gets older and the orange rind start to form.	Use greaseproof paper
Time	Keep the cheese in the warm room for 4 to 8 days	Age the cheese for 15–20 days	Wrap the cheese when you have a nice rind development and when the cheese is not too wet/sticky

When you space out the washing steps during the aging process, the Geotrichum will start to grow again on the surface of the cheese. Toward the end, when you stop washing two or three days before wrapping the cheese, a fine coating of a white mycelium will start to cover the orange rind. This is the Geotrichum growing again.

GOUDA CHEESE (RINDLESS CHEESE)

For Gouda cheese, you will rely mainly on the enzymes carried by the starter cultures, which is a mix of Lactococcus lactis subsp. lactis., Lactococcus lactis subsp. Cremoris and Streptococcus salivarius subsp.

thermophilus for the RA 021 from Danisco. We will also have the action of *Lactobacillus delbrueckii* subsp. *lactis* and *Lactobacillus helveticus* when you add LH100 from Danisco.

	If the cheese is brined	Primary aging	Secondary aging
Condition	Remove excess moisture in a drying room at 14–15°C/57–59°F with a relative humidity of 85% for approx. 24H	Age the cheese at 13°C/55°F in a vacuum bag	Age the cheese at 10°C/50°F in a vacuum bag
Aging care	-	-	-
Time	Immediately after the cheese is salted	Age the cheese for about 5 weeks	Age the cheese for another 6–8 weeks

TOMME DE SAVOIE TYPE CHEESE (NATURAL-RIND CHEESE)

Developing a natural rind on tomme cheese is an easy process. The best way to get a natural rind like the one on a Tomme de Savoie, you just have to buy a quarter of a wheel of a Tomme de Savoie (the real one) and place it in your aging chamber with the other cheese on which you are trying to develop a natural rind. The first growth of molds should appear within two weeks of the aging process. At this stage a primary layer of

ABOVE: Tomme cheese.

Geotrichum and *Mucor* should appear on the surface of the cheese. They will look light to dark gray. Within six weeks of the aging process, you may be able to see some yellow mold developing on the surface of the cheese as well as a red one at eight weeks.

	Aging	Wrap
Condition	Age the cheese at 8–10°C/46–50°F with a relative humidity of 98%	Cool off the cheese at 4°C/39°F for about 24H before wrapping the cheese to avoid condensation
Aging care	The cheese is turned regularly and the molds (*mucor*—cat's hair) is patted down by hand	-
Time	8 to 10 weeks	-

BLUE CHEESE WITH NO RIND DEVELOPMENT OUTSIDE

For the Blue cheese like a Roquefort-type cheese, you don't want any rind development on the outside, but we want some blue molds developing inside the cheese wheel. In order to prevent mold development on the surface of the cheese, you heavily coat the cheese with some coarse salt twice a day for two days. The rubbing action of the coarse salt on the cheese will prevent any microbiological activity on the surface of the cheese. Salting the cheese in a room at 20°C/68°F promotes the development of yeast inside the cheese paste, which will increase pH of the cheese paste, allowing the *Penicillium roqueforti* (blue mold) to develop.

	Primary aging	Secondary aging
Condition	Age the cheese at 12°C/54°F with a relative humidity of 90% for 15 to 20 days	Age the cheese at 2–4°C/36–39°F into a vacuum bag
Aging care	Brush off any mold development outside the cheese. Eight days into the aging process, take a plug away from the cheese wheel. If you don't have any blue development, pierce the cheese wheel with a needle. Repeat the same action in 15 days.	Once the cheese wheel has enough blue development, wrap the cheese wheel in foil fairly tightly to stop the development of *P. roqueforti*
Time	After the cheese has spent 2 days in the salting room.	Age the cheese for 2–3 months to promote the lipolysis (breakdown of fat)

How to make an aging environment suitable for the homestead cheesemaker

You can create your own aging enviroment for around $300. If you go online or look around for kitchen supply stores, you can find most of the elements easily. You will need:

- Wine/beer cooler (an inexpensive and easy way to maintain the proper aging temperature—approximate size)
- Straight shelf (to place cheese on for aging—approximate size and material recommended)
- Refrigerator thermostat (the probe measure and keep the temperature consistent inside the cooler)
- Hygro-thermoster (measure temperature and humidity inside the cooler
- Humidifier (maintain the relative humidity in the air to properly age the cheese—cool vapor is best)
- 24-hour mechanical timer (timer that turns power on and off of the humidifier at intervals to maintain the relative humidity in the enviroment)

Bellwether Farms

Nestled in the rolling hills of California's Sonoma Valley, Bellwether Farms was one of the first dairies in the United States to introduce sheep's milk cheeses to the American market. Ironically, when fifty-year-old Cindy Callahan, a retired nurse, purchased Bellwether back in 1986, she had no such intentions. In fact, there weren't even any sheep on the farm at the time. It wasn't until after two months of living on the farm that Cindy realized she needed some way of maintaining her pastures, so she bought a few sheep for the sole purpose of mowing the lawns. Things quickly changed at Bellwether, and it wasn't long before the sheep became the foundation for the successful cheesemaking business run by the Callahan family today.

It was good conversation and a glass of wine with a family friend three years after buying Bellwether that changed Cindy's perspective on her sheep forever. Her friend, of Syrian descent, explained that back in the Middle East, everyone milks sheep. It makes really good yogurt, really good milk, and really good cheese. After looking into the idea of a sheep dairy a little further, Cindy realized that the United States imported more than 60 million pounds of sheep's milk cheeses yearly. So, in addition to growing her flock and selling the meat as she had been doing for the past few years, Cindy decided to begin a new venture in the world of sheep's milk.

As she was in charge of the day-to-day care of the animals and needed help with the cheesemaking, Cindy easily convinced her son Liam, who was finishing a degree in political economy at the University of California, Berkeley, to join her full-time on the farm in 1990.

Liam had been helping his mom out on the farm on a part-time basis all along—shearing sheep, mending fences, and the like—but this time he jumped in with both feet, becoming the farm's Master cheesemaker. "I like having something that is concrete and made at the end of the day. In marketing or other industries you work with ideas, but there is no product every day. Cheesemaking fit really well with the way I am wired."

And after a couple of years, two trips to Italy (one by his mother, the other on his own) and experimenting with his own cheeses, Liam began creating the cheeses Bellwether is known for today. "I went to Italy to learn different techniques and to expand my knowledge base. But, the biggest influence of mine over the years has been my own cheesemaking. It's all trial and error."

Today, Bellwether Farms employs eighteen people, owns 200 sheep, and offers five different types of sheep's milk cheeses, including two raw sheep's milk cheeses—the smooth and full-flavored San Andreas and the semisoft Pepato, made with whole peppercorns—as well as three fresh cheeses. "Sheep's milk is beautiful milk. It's an expensive product, but it makes lovely stuff. It has nice flavors that are very distinct from goat's and cow's milk. I love working with it."

LEFT: Liam cutting the curd.

In addition to his sheep's-milk cheeses Liam also makes three different types of cow's-milk cheese using 3,000 pounds of cow's milk per week bought from a neighboring farmer. "Cow's milk prices fluctuate so much, but I always pay a flat price for our cow's milk, which can be up to three times the market price. This way, [the cow dairy] is always happy to see me. If there is a problem, they'll hold off their big milk trucks for me."

These days, the sheep dairy business on the West Coast has grown, and since 2004 Bellwether, California's original sheep dairy, is no longer the only one in the area. "We have been doing this for a while now. We have had more time to bring out the flavors in our cheeses. We have special flavors, but they may not be for everyone. They are cheeses that we like; they are consistent and the way we want them to be." To add to the high quality of the cheeses, Bellwether does not use any pesticides, pasture-raises their sheep with no use of hormones, and works with a cow dairy that uses the same principles.

Liam makes all his cheese to order and sells his sheep's-milk cheeses to local restaurants and high-end retailers. Carmody, one of Bellwether's cow's-milk cheeses named for the road that runs adjacent to the farm, and Liam's cow's-milk ricotta are sold nationally. "I like cheese. It's the best part of the job. I like the tradition of it. It's such an old craft with a tradition that goes way back."

All of Bellwether's products are award-winning, and include multiple first place medals from the American Cheese Society as well as medals in both cow and sheep's milk cheese categories at the World Cheese Awards.

Bellwether Farms

Sonoma Valley, California
Owners: **Liam and Cindy Callahan**
Cheesemaker: **Liam Callahan**
Email: **info@bellwetherfarms.com**
Website: **bellwethercheese.com**

Rustic Vegetable Cheese Frittata

Bellwether Farm's rustic veggie frittata is spectacular baked in a cast-iron pan. Every home cook has at least one well-seasoned skillet they couldn't imagine cooking without. This is the pan to use for this delicious recipe. Cast iron is highly valued for its many cooking properties; in this case, the pan's heat is evenly distributed, making it ideal for baking this frittata into its full rustic glory. *Serves 8*

2 T butter

3 T olive oil

1 large Spanish onion, thinly sliced

3 cloves of garlic, minced

2 small summer squash sliced ¼-inch thick

2 small zucchini, sliced ¼-inch thick

1 red bell pepper, seeded sliced ¼-inch strips

4 oz fresh cremini mushrooms, sliced

4 oz fresh oyster mushrooms, sliced

7 local fresh eggs

¼ C whipping cream

1 tsp coarse salt

1 tsp white pepper

2 C stale French bread cubes (¼-inch pieces)

3 oz crème fraîche

3 oz cream cheese

2 C grated Carmody Reserves cheese (a Manchego or Swiss will work well, too)

PHOTO CREDIT: *Olivia Farnham*

Preheat oven to 350°F (175°C).

Heat oil in a large pot over medium-high heat.

Add the onion, garlic, summer squash, zucchini, pepper, and mushrooms; sauté, stirring and tossing occasionally, until tender, 12–15 minutes.

While the veggies are cooking, whisk the eggs and cream together in a large mixing bowl. Season with salt and pepper.

Stir in the bread, crème fraîche, cream cheese, and grated cheese.

Fold sautéed vegetable into the egg mixture and stir well.

Heat a 10-inch cast-iron skillet over medium-high heat and melt butter in skillet.

Lower heat to medium-low; pour in egg and vegetable mixture.

With a wooden spoon, stir bottom of skillet, loosening cooked egg, for 1–2 minutes.

Take skillet off the heat and place in oven; bake for 45–50 minutes or until the frittata is firm to the touch, puffed, and golden brown. If it's browning too quickly, place a sheet of aluminum foil loosely over the top.

Serve warm atop field greens, such as arugula or mesclun and garnish with Red Onion Marmalade (see recipe on page 23). This is also perfectly delightful served at room temperature.

Try with . . .

Off the Vine: Try a Cru Beaujolais, fresh and delicious; the raspberry-mint aroma is a perfect accent to the cheesy baked goodness. Marcel Lapierre, Morgon 2008 has mastered this wine.

Appetite for Ale: Double IPA tend to have aromas of fruit and floral, like mango and pineapple on the nose. As it warms, more herbal notes come out along with a slight indication of the alcohol present in this brew. Try a Dreadnaught (Three Floyds Brewing Co, Munster, Indiana) or a Hopzilla Double IPA (Lawson's Finest, Warren, Vermont).

Cheese reference: left to right: Ayrshire Farmer's Cheese, La Luna, Queso, Acutney Mountain, Classic Blue, and Grafton Truckle.

PHOTO CREDIT: *Olivia Farnham*

Queso del Invi
sheep and co
Ielpi Major Fa
Putney, Vermo

Ayrshire Farmer's
Cheese
Ayrshire cow
Westfield Farm
Westfield, Massachusetts

Ascutney Mountain
raw cow
Cobb Hill
Hartland, Vermont

La Luna
cow goat
Blue Ledge Farm
Salisbury, Vermont

Classic Blue Log
goat
Westfield Farm
Westfield, Massachusetts

" The flavor of fresh Chèvre shifts with the seasons. It's tangy and citrusy in the late spring and summer when our goats are feasting on summer clover, cowpeas, millet, and sunflowers. In the fall and winter months, rye grass and clover fill the pastures, and fresh Chèvre takes on an earthy flavor. **"**

— JEREMY LITTLE, Cheesemaker, Sweet Grass Dairy

⑨

Core Cheese Makes

SO NOW YOU are ready to begin making cheese. You will find the process fascinating and at times frustrating. Give it time and attention, and you will succeed. The cheese makes at the beginning of this chapter are fairly easy to understand and follow. Queso is the perfect cheese to begin with. As you progress through these cheese makes you will find them increasingly more involved. Go back and review the information in the book; this will help clarify any questions you have during the cheesemaking process. One of the keys to successful cheesemaking is consistency and accuracy in measuring the raw ingredients; milk, creams, starter cultures, rennet, molds, and yeasts. For example, it can be difficult to measure small amounts of starter culture need for a specific cheese make, but you must be accurate.

The following recipes will indicate increments of measurement in both metric and teaspoon of measurement. However, the teaspoon measurement is an approximation and the metric measurement more exact. You can have as much as a 20 percent variation when using the teaspoon measurement. The metric system is the one we recommend you learn and use when developing your cheesemaking skills. Following the instructions accurately and consistently will ensure "best results" from the cheese makes in this chapter.

Fresh Cheeses

Fresh cheeses by definition are those that have not been aged or ripened. They are fresh, soft cheeses that are higher in moisture and lower in fat than other cheeses. Generally, fresh cheese is consumed quickly after production. Little equipment is needed to produce these types of cheeses, making them great for beginning cheesemakers.

Queso Blanco

This is a very simple recipe, and a great one to try first.

INGREDIENTS

6.8 L (1 gallon + 13 cups) skim milk	272 ml (1 cup + 2 ½ T) white vinegar
710 ml (3 cups) of heavy cream	25g (0.9 oz) fine salt without iodine

METHOD

1. In a double boiler, heat the milk and cream to 180°F. Stir constantly so mixture doesn't scald. Maintain the temperature for 5 minutes and remove pan from heat.
2. Add vinegar. Curd will begin to separate from whey.
3. Stir the curds and whey for 10–15 minutes. It will look like little cluster of fragile cheese curds in buttery-colored water.
4. Drain the curds into a colander that is lined with cheesecloth. Discard the whey.
5. Pour the curds into a clean bowl or into the cooking pot and add the salt. Stir evenly for 5 to 10 minutes to distribute evenly the salt.

6. Pour the curd into a form or mold (with holes to drain). If you wish, place a heavy weight on the mold. Leave overnight at room temperature.

7. Remove from the mold and store covered in the refrigerator for up to 2 weeks.

YIELD: Approximately 2 ½ pounds

TIME REQUIRED: 40 minutes

NOTE: Queso blanco fresco is a firm, moist cheese that holds its shape well when heated. Frying this cheese, called *queso para freir*, in a little bit of butter will soften but not melt it and is a wonderful way to taste queso's Hispanic roots.

1. We made this in a fish tank, so it's clear how the milk coagulates.

2. Draining the curd.

3. Molding the curds.

4. Pressing the curd.

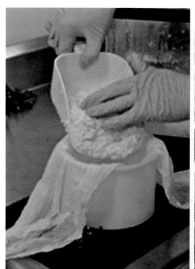

Fresh Chèvre

"Chèvre," French for "goat," refers to fresh, light-textured, rindless cheese make from pasteurized goat's milk. It is relatively simple to make and is delightfully smooth with a distinctively tangy flavor. The curd is softer and more delicate than curd of cow's milk, so the process requires a gentle hand. Chèvre comes in many shapes, including logs, small rounds and tiny cylinders, disks, or loose in bulk containers. Generally, Chèvre is vacuum-packed, but connoisseurs of fine artisan cheese seek out the more perishable leaf-wrapped and paper-wrapped rounds at specialty shops.

INGREDIENTS

18.9 L (5 gallons) pasteurized goat milk

4 ml (3/4 t) calcium chloride

1.89 Units of Flora Danica from Chr. Hansen or similar mix of homo-fermentative and heterofermentative mesophilic culture.

1 ml (1/4 t) calf rennet

Fine salt without iodine

Dried herbs or spices (optional)

METHOD

1. In a stainless steel pot heat the milk slowly to 70°F/21°C. Stir constantly so mixture doesn't scald.

2. Remove from heat, add the calcium chloride mixture, and stir to combine.

3. Sprinkle in the culture and then stir gently to combine. Maintain the milk at 18–65–70°F/ 20°C.

4. Add the animal rennet when the pH reaches 6.3 (it should take approximately 6 hours). Stir well for 1 minute, cover pot, and maintain at 65–70°F/18–20°C. Let stand until the pH reaches 6.35–6.45 (it will take approximately another 10–12 hours). Do not move or agitate the pot while the curd sets.

5. Ladle the curd into molds on the draining mat. Note: the curd should look like a firm yogurt. Allow the whey to drain out and away from the molds. Drain for 24 hours at 18–65–70°F/ 20°C.

6. Unmold the cheese rounds and place on ripening mat. Hand salt by sprinkling 1.4 percent of fine salt per cheese weight on all sides. Place cheese in drying area and allow drying for 24 hours, turning once or twice for even drying surface.

7. Coat cheese with herbs or spices before wrapping (optional). Wrap in specialty cheese paper or wax paper and then plastic wrap over that. Refrigerate. It will keep for 2 weeks or so.

YIELDS: Approximately 6.5–8.5 pounds (depending on the moisture of the cheese after demolding)

REQUIRED TIME: 3 days till final results

NOTE: Chèvre is very versatile in the kitchen. It's spreadable, so slice medallions onto seeded baguette rounds, heat under the broiler, add a dollop of apricot jam. Or crumble flavored pepper- or herb-coated Chèvre into salads, or add as a topping for pizza.

Cheese to go

Ricotta technically isn't a cheese at all. It's a by-product of cheesemaking. The name "ricotta" means "recooked" in Italian (from the Latin *recoctus*). When milk is coagulated to make cheese, the curds are pressed together to make the cheese, and the whey is drained off. Long ago, the leftover whey was simply fed to the pigs, a practice still continued today. But somewhere along the line, someone discovered that the whey contained proteins and milk solids that would coagulate under high enough heat and with the presence of an acid (like vinegar)—"recooking" the whey.

What Is Ash?

Ash is used in cheesemaking for both aesthetic and practical reasons. It is as much about tradition as it is the science of cheesemaking. Ash originally came from the charcoal of oak trees, which was the tradition in the Loire Valley of France. Ash has many purposes in the cheesemaking process. It offers protection for the cheese when it is used on the outside surface in the aging process. It's especially helpful to lactic curd cheeses such as goat cheese, helping to neutralize the surface acidity of the cheese, which allows mold and yeasts to successfully grow and develop the rind. Visually it's very striking as well. A dark line of ash running through the middle of a pure white cheese is very stunning. Ash used for aesthetic appeal today has its roots in the traditional use of ash. The farmer would cover the leftover cheese curd from the first cheese make with a layer of ash to protect it from flies and insects. When the second milking was complete, the curd from that make was added on top, and the cheese was finished. The French Morbier is a great example of ash's visual appeal. Today ash is made from particles of carbonized vegetable matter.

ABOVE: Ash being shaken on Bonne Bouche at Vermont Butter and Cheese Creamery.

ABOVE: Layers of ash in Humboldt Fog from Cypress Grove.

Soft-ripened Cheeses

The soft-ripened cheese category includes many cheeses that fall between the fresh and washed cheese families, though many soft-ripened cheeses are washed as part of the production. Soft-ripened cheeses generally lend themselves to consumption within a month or two of production. They have a high percentage of moisture in the interior paste; this create the smooth, creamy, gooey texture that becomes more pronounced as the cheese ripens. Soft-ripened cheeses like Camemberts and triple-creams fall into the subcategory of mold-ripened cheese. The milk for mold-ripened cheese is inoculated with molds and yeasts at the time of the make or sprayed onto the rind after production, causing a light coating of fizz to develop during *affinage*. These good microorganisms break down the paste of the cheese and help to develop the flavor profile.

Camembert

Flora Danica is here to acidify the cheese, MD089 is here to enhance the flavor of the cheese flavor in order to produce some nutty flavor, the TA054 is here to give the cheese a creamy texture, the KL71 is here to de-acidify the surface of the cheese to allow the development of the Geotrichum, the Geotrichum is here to control the growth of the Penicillium, and Pencillium is here for the rind and flavor development of the cheese.

INGREDIENTS

17.0 L (4 gallons + 8 cups) skim milk

1.9 L (8 cup) heavy cream

2 ml (1/2 t) calcium chloride

1.7 Units of Flora Danica from Chr. Hansen or similar mix of homo-fermentative and heterofermen-tative mesophilic culture

0.09 DCU of MD089 from Danisco or similar heterofermentative mesophilic culture

0.57 DCU of TA054 from Danisco or equivalent

0.06 Dose of KL71 from Danisco

0.04 Dose of Geo 17 from Danisco

0.11 Dose of ABL or Neige from Danisco

4 ml (3/4 t) calf rennet

Fine salt without iodine

METHOD

1. Add the calcium chloride to the milk, and stir to combine.
2. Heat the milk to 36°C/97°F. Add the culture and stir to combine. Cover, maintain at 36°C/97 °F, and allow to ripen until the milk pHreaches 6.45±0.05.

RIGHT: A light coating of fuzz develops on this Camembert ring during aging.

3. Add the rennet and stir well for 1 minute. Cover and let set at 36°C/97°F. Observe the flocculation time. Multiply the flocculation time by two, which will give you the hardening time of the gel. It allows you to estimate the time to cut the gel. However, the most important thing is to cut the gel at the right firmness.

4. Cut the curd into 2 cm/¾-inch cubes. After cutting, let curds settle for 5 minutes. Stir the curd manually and gently for 5 minutes. Let the curd rest for 5 minutes. Stir the curd again for five minutes. finally, let the curd settle again for 5 minutes. The most important thing is that the curds are not too wet or to dry, therefore the resting and stirring can be modulated until the desire curd texture is obtained.

5. Pour off approximately 30 percent of whey based on the initial volume (5.7L/1.5 gallons). Pour the curd and whey mixture into the molds.

6. Flip the cheese at 1, 3, 5, and 8 hours after molding the cheese curd. Monitor the pH of the cheese and the temperature of the room during drainage and compare it to the reference point.

TARGET PH AND TEMPERATURE DURING DRAINING

	Curd pH	Room temperature
Molding	6.30 ±0.05	27 ±1°C /81 ±1°F
Molding + 1H	6.00 ±0.05	27 ±1°C /81 ±1°F
Molding + 3H	5.7 ±0.05	25 ±1°C /77 ±1°F
Molding + 5H	5.45 ±0.05	25 ±1°C /77 ±1°F
Molding + 8H	5.10 ±0.05	23 ±1°C /73 ±1°F
Demolding	4.90 ±0.05	20 ±1°C /68 ±1°F

7. The next day remove the cheese from the molds. Then add 1.9 percent of salt by cheese weight. Make sure to distribute the salt evenly between the top and the bottom.

8. Age the cheeses 10–15 days at 13–140°C/55–570°C with a relative humidity of 90–92 percent. Turn the cheeses every day during the aging process. Your Camembert is ripe when the mold is fully bloomed on the outside of the cheese.

YIELDS: Approximately 6 pounds

REQUIRED TIME: Make time 4–5 hours excluding flipping and aging time

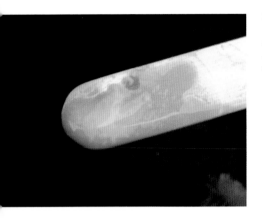

LEFT: Flocculation after the addition of the calf rennet.

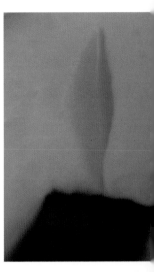

RIGHT: Check firmness of the curd before cutting.

BELOW: Salt rubbed on the surface of the young fresh cheese.

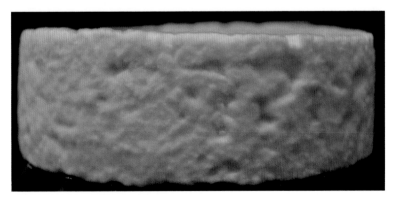

ABOVE: Appearance of the molds six days into the aging period. The cheese will be fully bloomed in another four to five days.

Reblochon-type

Washed-rind cheeses are typically smeared with a solution of salt water and friendly bacteria. Washing helps to break down the cheese curd and retain moisture. Some cheesemakers wash their cheese with local spirits of the region, such as beer, wine, or hard cider, producing a true *terroir* cheese. Smearing the cheese as it ages also helps to develop the pungent exterior, creating a deep flavor profile for this type of cheese. Washed-rind cheeses are often a turnoff because of this strong aroma from the rind, but beneath that sticky, orange exterior is a soft, thick delicious paste that is a brilliant contrast on the palate. NOTE: Heat-treated water is water that has been brought to a boil, cooled off, and kept in sanitized container.

INGREDIENTS

17.0 L (4 gallons + 8 cups) skim milk	1.89 DCU of MY 800 from Danisco or equivalent
1.9 L (8 cups) heavy cream	0.02 Dose of PLA from Danisco or equivalent
2 ml (1/2 t) calcium chloride	4 ml (3/4 t) calf rennet

BRINE

3.8 L (1 gallon) heat-treated water	Add 4 ml (3/4 t) calcium chloride
1.4 Kg (3 lbs) fine salt without iodine	Add vinegar until the pH of the brine drops down to 5.3

SMEARING SOLUTION

0.9 L (3 cup + 12 T + 2 ½ t) heat-treated water	40 g (1.4 oz) fine salt without iodine
	2 Doses of PLA

METHOD:

1. Heat the milk to 34.5°C/94°F. Add the thermophilic starter culture, the PLA (mix of aging culture), the calcium chloride, and stir to combine.

2. Allow to ripen until the milk pH reaches 6.45±0.05. Add the animal rennet and stir well for 1 minute. Cover and let set at 34.5°C/94°F. Observe the flocculation time. Multiply the flocculation (10–15 minutes) time by one, which will give you the hard-

ening time of the gel. Remember, the most important thing is to cut the gel the correct firmness.

3. Cut the curd into 2 cm / ¾-inch cubes. At end of cut, let curds settle for 5 minutes. Stir the curd manually and gently for 10 minutes. Let the curd rest for 5 minutes. Stir the curd again for five minutes. Finally, let the curd settle again for 5 minutes. The most important thing is to have curds that are not too wet or too dry. The resting and stirring can be modulated until the desired curd texture is obtained.

4. Remove approximately 35 percent of the whey based on the initial volume (6.6L/1.75 gallons) with a siphon or small measuring cup. Pour the curd-and-whey mixture into the molds. Press the cheese with 15 g/cm²/0.21 pound per square inch for 90 minutes. After 30 minutes of pressing, flip the cheese and press again.

5. Flip the cheese at 1, 3, 5, and 8 hours after molding the cheese curd. Monitor the pH of the cheese and the temperature of the room during drainage and compare it to the reference point.

TARGET PH AND TEMPERATURE DURING DRAINING

	Curd pH	Room temperature
Molding	6.35 ±0.05	27 ± 1°C /81 ± 1°F
Molding + 1H	6.10 ±0.05	27 ± 1°C /81 ± 1°F
Molding + 3H	5.7 ±0.05	25 ± 1°C /77 ± 1°F
Molding + 5H	5.40 ±0.05	25 ± 1°C /77 ± 1°F
Molding + 8H	5.35 ±0.05	23 ± 1°C /73 ± 1°F
Demolding	5.3 ±0.05	20 ± 1°C /68 ± 1°F

6. Allow to set overnight so pH falls around 5.3. Remove the cheese from the form and brine the cheese for 90 minutes if the cheese has a diameter of 14cm/5.51 in and a height of 3.5cm/1.4 in.

7. Place the cheese onto an aging rack and let it dry for 4 days at relative humidity of 98 percent at a temperature of 17–18°C/63–64°F. In a few a days the rind will have developed a coating of *Geotricum*. It's now ready to be smeared.

8. Make a smearing solution by combining the water and salt and adding some more aging culture. Don't forget to mix the water and salt first, otherwise you will kill the culture. Smear the cheese by rubbing the solution completely over the surface of the cheese.

9. Age the cheeses 15 days at 12–13°C/54–55°C with a relative humidity of 96 percent. Turn the cheeses every day during the aging process.

YIELDS: Approximately 5.6 pounds

REQUIRED TIME: Make time 3½ hours excluding aging time

ABOVE: Mold lineup before sending the cheese curd-and-whey mixture at the National Dairy School in La Roche sur Foron.

ABOVE: Cheese press for Reblochon at the National Dairy School in La Roche sur Foron.

BELOW: Cheese brine for Reblochon at the National Dairy School in La Roche sur Foron.

ABOVE: Reblochon cheese at the beginning of the aging process at the National Dairy School in La Roche sur Foron.

BELOW: Reblochon cheese toward the end of the aging process at the National Dairy School in La Roche sur Foron.

Semi-hard Cheeses

Semi-hard cheese has a texture that feels firmer than the soft-ripened cheese category and contains even less moisture. With semi-hard cheeses the curd has been cut into a smaller grain, which in turn releases more whey from the curd. Many cheeses in this category are brined during the make process, adding to their overall flavor development. There is wide variety of semi-hard or firm cheeses; examples are: Colby, Gouda, Brick, and Montasio.

Gouda

Washed-curd cheeses such as Gouda are cooked by replacing the discarded whey with hot water. The method of rinsing the lactose from the curd helps to delay the acidification and prevent the cheese from becoming sour and to have a brittle texture. This process is also key to the development of this type of cheese's typical smooth texture and clean, mild flavor profile.

INGREDIENTS

17.3 L (4 gallons + 9 C + 4 ½ T) skim milk	1.18 DCU of RA021 from Danisco or equivalent
1.6 L (6 cups + 11 ½ t) heavy cream	0.14 DCU of LH100 from Danisco or equivalent
2 ml (1/2 t) calcium chloride	3.5 ml (3/4 t) calf rennet

BRINE

3.8 L (1 gallon) heat-treated water	Add some vinegar until the pH of the brine drop down to 5.2
1.4 Kg (3 lbs) salt	
Add 4 ml (3/4 t) calcium chloride	

METHOD

1. Heat milk to 32°C/90°F and add the calcium chloride, then add your starter culture. Allow ripening until the milk pH reaches 6.60–6.65 (approximately 1–2 hours).

2. Add the animal rennet and stir well for 1 minute. Cover and let set at 32°C/90°F. Observe the flocculation time. Multiply the flocculation (20–25 minutes) time by one, which will give you the hardening time of the gel. Remember, it is most important is to cut the gel always at the right firmness.

3. Cut the curd into pea-size cubes and then let stand for 5 minutes, then stir the curds for 30 minutes.

4. Drain off 30 percent (5.7 L/1.5 gallons) of the whey and replace with 25 percent (4.7L/1.25 gasllons) of heat-treated water at 32°C/90°F (based on the initial volume). Slowly stir, and increase the heat to 37.5°C/99.5°F over a period of 20 minutes and stir for another 30 minutes.

5. Next allow the curd to settle for 5 minutes, then slightly prepress the curd under whey for 10–15 minutes, then remove the whey from the cheese vat.

6. Cut the cheese mat in the cheese vat in a block and fill up the cheese molds lined with a cheesecloth. Start to press slowly up to 200g/cm² /2.84 lbs per square inch overnight.

TARGET PH AND TEMPERATURE DURING DRAINING

	Curd pH	Room temperature
Molding	6.50 ±0.05	20 ± 1°C /68 ± 1°F
Molding + 1H	6.10 ±0.05	20 ± 1°C /68 ± 1°F
Molding + 3H	5.15 ±0.05	20 ± 1°C /68 ± 1°F
Demolding	5.10 ±0.05	20 ± 1°C /68 ± 1°F

7. Remove the cheese from the mold and brine the cheese for 3 hours 30 minutes/pound. Allow the cheese to air-dry until you have no more excess moisture on the surface of the cheese.

8. Vacuum pack the cheese and age it at 14°C/57°F for 4–6 weeks and store it at 10°C/50°F in its vacuum bag for 1–2 months.

YIELDS: Approximately 5.1 pounds

REQUIRED TIME: Make time 3–4 hours excluding aging time

Tomme de Savoie–type (natural rind)

Tomme-style cheese is a semi-hard cheese with a deliciously nutty flavor and a smooth paste that melts in your mouth. The grayish hard, powdery rind has an earthy aroma and is usually speckled with many types of beneficial flora. During aging some yellow or red molds can appear on it. Its paste is white to pale yellow with small openings and in France is exclusively manufactured with cow's milk. It was once considered the poor man's cheese, as it was made with skimmed milk during the nineteenth century. The French privileged demanded full-fat cheeses, and fatty tommes were reserved for the fat cats.

INGREDIENTS

17.0 L (4 gallons + 8 cups) skim milk

1.9 L (8 cups) heavy cream

2 ml (1/2 t) calcium chloride

0.71 DCU of MA011 from Danisco or equivalent

0.24 DCU of MD088 from Danisco or equivalent

0.24 DCU of TA054 from Danisco or equivalent

0.04 Dose of LBC82 from Danisco or equivalent

3 ml (1/2 t) calf rennet

Coarse salt

1. Heat milk to 32°C/90°F and add the calcium chloride, then add your starter culture. Allow ripening until the milk pH reaches 6.55–6.60 (approximately 2½–3 hours).

2. Add the animal rennet and stir well for 1 minute. Cover and let set at 32°C/90°F. Observe the flocculation time. Multiply the flocculation (15–20 minutes) time by 1, which will give you the hardening time of the gel. It is most important to cut the gel at the correct firmness. If you wait too long with sheep's milk, it will be impossible to cut the gel.

3. Cut the curd into 1cm/0.4-inch pieces and let rest for 1 minute. Gently start to stir the curd for 40 minutes while slowly raising the temperature to 36°C/97°C (increase the temperature by one degree every minute).

4. To transfer the curds to the mold, dip your cheesecloth into the vat and capture the curd, gently. Then place the cheesecloth into the mold. Stack two to three molds on each other in order to have

a slight pressure on the cheese. During the drainage of the cheese curds, keep the mold in a room without drafts at a temperature of 20°C/68°F.

5. Remove the cheese from the mold and salt heavily the entire surface with 2.5 percent salt per cheese weight using coarse salt.

6. Age the cheeses between 6–8 weeks at 12–14°C/54–57°C with a relative humidity of 96 percent. Turn the cheeses every day at the beginning, and pat down the cat's hair (*mucor*) during the aging process.

YIELDS: Approximately 5 pounds

REQUIRED TIME: Make time 3–4 hours excluding aging time

ABOVE: Stacks of Gouda being aged.   ABOVE: Tommè de Savoie.

Blue Cheese

It is commonly fabled that Blue cheese was created by accident and has been around since Roman times. The "curd" on the street is that bread was left to mold in the cheese cave of a local cheesemaker in Aveyron, France. Blue spores grew on the bread and commingled with the cheese in the cave. Voilà! The result was none other than the Roquefort we know and love today. The process for creating the distinctive pattern of blue veins in the interior of the cheese comes from piercing the cheese with long needles. The blue mold requires a tiny bit of oxygen to flourish, and the deep penetration of the needle helps to create the pathways for the blueing to take place. Blues can be difficult to master; they require attention to detail for the proper aging environment.

INGREDIENTS:

18.0 L (5 gallons) pasteurized sheep milk	0.04 Dose of PJ from Danisco
4 ml (3/4 t) calcium chloride	3 ml (1/2 t) calf rennet
1.5l Unit of CHN 11 from Chr. Hansen	24.5 g (0.9 oz) fine salt without iodine
0.38 DCU of LM057 from Danisco	Coarse salt

METHOD:

1. Heat milk to 32°C/90°F. Add the starter, then the mold mix well.
2. Allow to ripen until the milk pH reaches 6.40±0.05 (approximately 4–5 hours). Add the animal rennet and stir well for 1 minute. Cover and let set at 32°C/90°F. Observe the flocculation time. Multiply the flocculation time (10–12 minutes) by 0.42, which will give you the hardening time of the gel. Remember, the most important thing is to cut the gel always at the right firmness. If you wait too long with sheep milk, it will be impossible to cut the gel.
3. Cut the curd into 1cm/0.4-inch cubes. Let set for 30 seconds to 1 minute. Stir the curds for 10 minutes. Then remove 10 percent of whey (1.85L/0.5 gallon). Stir the curd again for 10 minutes. Remove 10 percent of whey (1.85L/0.5 gallon). Stir 10 min. Remove all the whey. The most important is to have curds that are not too wet or too dry. The resting and stirring can be modulated until the desired curd texture is obtained.

4. Add salt to the cheese curds. Dry stir for 2–3 minutes, allowing a homogeneous salt distribution.

5. Pour the curd into the molds. Sprinkle the curds in the mold, allowing the formation of mechanical holes.

6. Flip the cheese at ½, 1, 3, 5 and 8 hours after molding the cheese curd. Monitor the pH of the cheese and the temperature of the room during drainage and compare it to the reference point.

TARGET PH AND TEMPERATURE DURING DRAINING

	Curd pH	Room temperature
Molding	6.35–6.15	28 ± 1°C /82 ± 1°F
Molding + 1/2H	6.30–6.10	28 ± 1°C /82 ± 1°F
Molding + 1H	6.10–5.90	27 ± 1°C /81 ± 1°F
Molding + 3H	5.60–5.40	25 ± 1°C /77 ± 1°F
Molding + 5H	5.30–5.10	23 ± 1°C /73 ± 1°F
Molding + 8H	5.10–4.90	20 ± 1°C /68 ± 1°F
Demolding	5.0–4.80	20 ± 1°C /68 ± 1°F

7. Remove the cheese from the mold; rub and coat the cheese surface with coarse salt twice a day for two days in a room at 20°C/68°F.

8. Age the cheeses 15–20 days at 12°C/54°C with a relative humidity of 90 percent. Turn the cheeses every day during the aging process. Make sure to store the cheese sideways so the air can go through the holes when the cheese is pierced.

9. After 8 days into the aging process, remove a cheese sample using a cheese trier. Check for any blue development in the sample. If bluing is not present or suffiicent, use a 2–4mm/0.08–0.16-inch sanitized needle to poke some holes throughout the cheese wheel. Check again 15 days into the aging process for the development of the blue mold. If the blue is not developing enough, pierce the cheese a second time. Once you have enough blue development, wrap the cheese wheel in foil. Make sure that the foil is really tight to the cheese wheel. Then store the cheese in cold storage at 2–4°C/36–39°F for 4–5 months.

YIELDS: Approximately 10.5 pounds

REQUIRED TIME: Make time 1½ hours excluding ripening and aging time

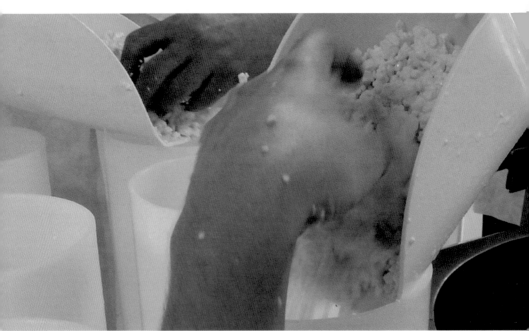

ABOVE: Molding the cheese curds into Blue cheese.

ABOVE: Blue cheese just after unmolding. Piercing will be done in about ten days, allowing oxygen to enter the body of the cheese, signaling the *Penicillium roqueforti* to do its dance.

ABOVE: Salting the Blue cheese wheel.

ABOVE: Piercing the Blue cheese wheel.

The Blues from
Rogue River
Creamery.

❝ A bit of sweetness complements most cheeses and a dab of honey has the ability to tame a wild cheese. I keep several types on hand and encourage guests to mix and match. A Couple of my favorite combos are truffle honey with firm sheep's cheese and floral honeys with Blues. ❞

—LOUIS RISOLI, Maître d' and Fromager, I'E, Boston MA

⑩

Building a Cheese Board

EVER ARRIVE HOME with a beautiful piece of cheese you splurged on at the farmers' market or specialty shop, only to find you don't really know how to handle it? There are a multitude of reasons that drew you to purchase this particular cheese: its look, its smell, its taste. Maybe the cheesemaker told you the story behind this wedge of cheese. Whatever connection you've made to this cheese and its subsequent purchase is the same conviviality you will want to pass along to friends and family who join you in tasting it. To maintain the integrity of the cheese, the quality and your care of it are essential to bringing the cheese to its full potential for enjoyment.

Cheese is molded into many forms. Wheels, truckle, and pyramids— each cheese has a shape and a special way to cut it. Cutting the wedge correctly will help to showcase the qualities of the cheese and enhance

LEFT: PHOTO CREDIT: *Ora Moore*

the flavor profile. When tasting cheese, you want to be able to taste the entire spectrum of flavor inherent in each cheese slice. All cheese tastes different closer to the rind than it will in the center; it's simply the aging process. As cheese ages from the outside in, you will notice much variation in the texture, taste, and finish of each slice of cheese. Cutting the cheese correctly to showcase these nuances is interesting and informative. See the cutting chart in this sections to help demystify "how to cut" cheese.

You will find helpful charts in this chapter to guide you in cutting and plating your cheese and help you select from a list of tasty accompaniments to enrich your tasting experience. Whey Wheels are flavor cue lexicons for cow's, goat's, and sheep's milk cheese: they provide flavor cues when tasting cheese, helping you to develop some fun and informed cheese vocabulary.

The Whey Wheels in this section are to remind you of the cheese classification you have been studying: The five categories are: fresh cheese, soft-ripened cheese, semi-hard cheese, hard cheese, and Blue cheese. Think of these lexicons as a sensory dictionary of cheese. It will help build your nomenclature in the industry, ultimately enabling you to communicate simply and effectively about the flavor profile of a cheese.

To read the chart: The Whey Wheel starts at 12 o'clock and moves clockwise. There are five small circles on the wheel that identify a cheese from each of the cheese family classifications.

Start by identifying the center of the circle as the breed of animal and the milk used to make the cheese. The cheeses are labeled at the center of the smaller bubbles around the outside of the large wheel there are five on each wheel. The smallest circles are descriptive flavor cues generally associated with that cheese. This is a quick way for you to capture some cheese vocabulary when "talking cheese" with your guests.

NOTE: Taste and smell are two distinct sensory receptors. Taste is very easy to describe, because there are just five tastes; salty, bitter, sour, sweet, and umami, which is a Japanese word meaning "savory"—the flavor is sometimes described as "meatiness" or "deliciousness." However, when you're describing cheese, taste and smell are always going to be intermixed. Here "flavor" refers to the joint effect of the cheese's taste and smell. So taste is in-the-mouth feel and smell is on-the-nose smell... there you go—a few more sensory terms.

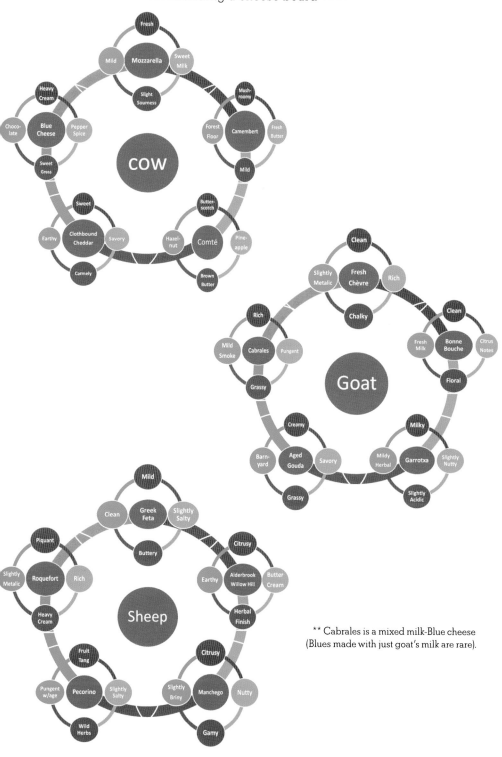

** Cabrales is a mixed milk-Blue cheese
(Blues made with just goat's milk are rare).

Cheese Cutting Chart

The chart below is a helpful guide for cutting cheese and bringing the cheese flavor profile to its full potential.

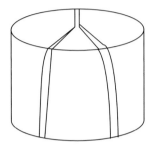

Small cylinder cheese, cut down center for long wedge, turn on side and slice. (examples: triple creams, Saint André, or goat crottins). Washed-rind (example: Petit Basque).

Small wheels of bloomy rind, cut from center out (like pie) (examples: Camembert or Bonne Bouche). Smaller washed-rind wheels (example: Stinking Bishop).

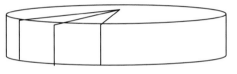

Designed by:
Jody Farnham

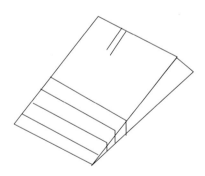

Wedge with hard cheese texture, cut across to create "fingers" (examples: Comté or Ossau Iraty). Natural-rind and clothbound cheddars.

Pyramid-or cone-shaped cheese. Cut down center for long wedges (examples: Valencay or Piper's Pyramid and Cerney).

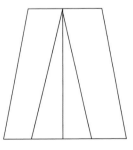

Cheeses in wooden box or wrapped in bark: Slice the top off or make a hole for scooping. (examples: Époisses or Saint-Marcellin or a very ripe Winnemere).

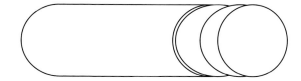

Smaller cylindrical cheeses, cut small discs; plain waxed dental floss works well. (examples: fresh Chèvre log, Sainte-Maure, and the classic Blue log).

Flat square cheeses; cut triangular wedges. (examples: bloomy-rind Robiola or washed-rind Le Brin).

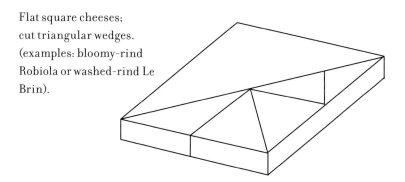

Creating a cheese board for a cocktail hour is simple and will create a focal point for your entertaining. Cheese is an engaging subject for everyone and knowing just a few fun tidbits about the cheese you are serving can be a great conversation starter. If you make special

purchases of local cheeses and accompaniments like bread, berry compote, or wine, be sure to ask the vendors about the product, become informed, and make a connection to them so you have a little story to tell
when entertaining. That's informed entertainment!

Diversity is key in selecting cheeses for your cheese board or cheese
course with dinner. Choose cheeses made with different milks and from
the different classifications of cheese; this will ensure everyone finds
something they enjoy. Start with three to five different types of cheese
for your first time or two. Once you feel comfortable you will have a difficult time choosing which cheeses to select for your entertaining. You
will want to try them all!

When tasting cheese, start with the milder, fresh cheeses at the
beginning and move toward the stronger, more pungent ones. Cheese
selection should include first a fresh cheese like a Chèvre, next a soft-
ripened cheese, like a Petite Brie or Camembert. For the third cheese
choose one from the semi-hard family, like a Tomme de Savoie or an aged
Gouda. The last cheese selection should be one that has a little or big
kick to it. This will allow for showing off the marked differences from

BELOW: Creating a cheese board for a cocktail hour is simple and will create a focal
point for your entertaining. Knowing just a few fun tidbits about the cheese you are serving can be a great conversation starter.

the first cheese to the last cheese. Choose Cahel Blue or St. Agur from the Blue family as your last selection. These four types of cheese offer the perfect balance of texture, taste, and intensity for your cheese board.

Cheese is just the beginning of a successful cheese board; complement the cheese with something sweet, savory, salty, and a bit unusual, like maple-flavored kettle corn. Go beyond the basics of tasting just cheese and select a few accompaniments that have varied flavors and textures. For example: toasted nuts, fresh fruit like apples and pears, a savory compote, charcuterie (cured and salted meats), and dark chocolate, of course! You only need a handful of each of these items to create a richer tasting experience. Serve them on the same platter as the cheeses, so your guests know they are meant to be consumed together. Ramekins work well for wet accompaniments like Italian brined olives and French cornichon pickles.

The presentation of the cheese board is a powerful tool for engaging your guest to dive in and taste. Use your imagination and look for unusual platters, wooden boards, rattan mats, inverted trays, cake pedestal, a piece of slate left over from the roof. Cater your serving ware to the occasion—polishing up the antique silver platter provides a classic French cheese-cart feel. A large piece of white birch bark is striking set with little pyramids of bloomy-rind cheese and sides of berries and herbs. The perfect beverage pairing is hot mulled cider. Remember your old cake pedestal with the glass top, perfect for displaying a small cheese selection. The point is to make it your own and have fun doing so!

If you feel the standard Cheddar is missing add that as well. Cheddar is in the hard cheese family and would be placed in the tasting disposition of your cheese board after the semi-hard and before the Blue. A few words about cutting and placing the cheese on your board: It's nice to slice a few pieces of cheese off the wedge or cut a piece or two from the wheel; this provides a look inside the cheese and gives your guests easy access to a taste of the cheese. Alternatively, to keep things fun and interactive allow your guests to cut and taste their own cheeses as they wish. Place small knives or forks (forks work well with crumbly Blue cheese) by each of the cheeses. Self-guided tastings are wonderful, as you can mix and match the cheese and the accompaniments to find the ultimate pairing.

Savory Cherry Compote

To prepare the cheeses for tasting, take them out of the refrigerator and place on your board for at least one hour at room temperature. This will warm them and enhance their flavor profile and will allow their texture to become soft and supple on the palate. Leave them in their original paper wrapper or foil until service; this will reduce air-drying on the surface and will hold some cheese formats together. If you cut into a ripe Brie cheese to soon, your guests will be chasing it all over the counter.

3 T olive oil	1 T fresh thyme leaves, stemmed
2 T minced shallots (or finely chopped red onion)	2 T sweet clover honey
3 C pitted cherries, quartered	¾ C red wine (like Zinfandel or Syrah) or Tawny Port
½ C walnuts, chopped and toasted	2 T cider vinegar
½ C pecans, chopped and toasted	Salt and pepper to taste
1 T fresh rosemary, minced	

Heat olive oil in a large, heavy saucepan over medium heat.

Add shallots and sauté for 2–3 minutes.

Turn heat to medium-low and add the nuts, rosemary, and cherries, stirring to combine evenly.

Cook until cherries are soft, 5–6 minutes, and stir to keep from sticking. Sprinkle in a bit of salt and black pepper.

Next, add the wine, vinegar, and honey, and bring to a boil for 1–2 minutes.

Reduce heat and cook down until mixture becomes thick, with a syrupy consistency. Add fresh thyme leaves and stir.

Remove from heat and cover, then let stand 15 minutes. Serve warm. Refrigerate in glass jar with lid for up to 2 weeks.

YIELD: Makes about 2 cups

TIME: 30 minutes

LEFT: This aromatic compote made with fresh stone fruit, savory herbs, and heavenly red wine combines for an excellent accompaniment to many cheeses. Try complementing the nutty goodness of both with an aged sheep's-milk cheese like Manchego, or dollop the cherry compote warm on top of baby Chèvre crottins.

Candied Grapefruit Rinds

2 grapefruits peeled (red or pink)	1 C white sugar
1 C water	½ C light corn syrup
½ C honey	Sanding sugar (for rolling)*

Place grapefruit peels in a saucepan and cover them with water. Bring to a boil over medium-high heat, then reduce the heat to simmer. Cook for about 25 minutes, or until the peels are soft. Drain the peels. Remove the white pithy layer, leaving just the skin. Slice the peel into thin strips.

In a heavy saucepan, mix sugar, 1 cup water, honey, and corn syrup; bring to a boil over high heat. Reduce heat to a simmer, and add the strips of grapefruit peel. Cook until they become translucent, about 45–50 minutes.

Remove the strips with a slotted spoon, and drain them. Allow the candied rind to cool just enough for it to be handled. Sprinkle a thick layer of coarse sugar onto a large plate. Spoon the peel strips onto the sugar, and toss them with a fork to coat them evenly. Transfer the strips to a large sheet of wax paper, and let them dry for about 1–2 hours.

Store in single layers on wax paper in a cool place. Keeps for weeks.

YIELD: 3 cups of rinds
TIME: 1 hour

BELOW: Grapefruit peel can be deliciously and simply preserved to create a sweet pairing for soft-ripened cheeses, highlighting the sweet citrus notes of lemon and balancing the tangy milk flavors in these cheeses.

* Sanding or coarse sugar has large crystals that reflect light and give the product a sparkling appearance. For something special, dip one end of each rind in melted dark chocolate.

Dovè Spicy Nuts

(adapted from Pam Clark's recipe)

3 C mixed nuts	1 T smoked cayenne pepper, heaping
1 egg white	1 tsp cinnamon
1 T orange juice	½ tsp ginger
⅔ C white sugar	½ tsp allspice
1 T grated orange rind	½ tsp salt

Heat oven to 275°F. In a large bowl combine egg white, orange juice, orange rind, and spices; mix well.

Add the nuts and toss to coat well.

Place parchment paper on two standard cookie sheets and spread the nuts out evenly on the sheets. Bake for 35 minutes, stirring and turning the nuts every 15 minutes, until light brown.

Note: The nuts will appear to still be wet and sticky, but remove from oven and allow to cool. They will become crispy as they cool down. Place in airtight container for storage.

YIELD: Makes 4 cups
TIME: 45–50 minutes

For a rustic
touch to
your cheese
board,
add fresh
herbs and
wildflowers
from the
garden.

PHOTO CREDIT:: *Olivia Farnham*

CHEESE PLEASERS

Family of Cheese	Sweet	Savory	Salty	Go Big
Fresh Cheese Fresh Chèvre, feta, ricotta, quark	Clover honey Baked pears	*Roasted Beet Salad Cider jelly w/ fresh thyme	Toasted pecans Saucisson sec (French salami)	Apricot preserve and ground black pepper
Soft-ripened Cheese Saint-Marcellin, Bijou, Camembert, Les Freres	Watermelon rind Maple syrup	*Tomato Basil Jam *Cherry Compote	Duck comfit Dilly beans	*Candied Grapefruit Rind Edamame, lightly salted
Semihard Cheese Tomme de Savoie, Monterey Jack, Gouda	Dried plums and cranberries Blood oranges	Grilled fennel (sliced thin) Classic country ham	Brined olives Mixed nut brittle	Sautéed mushroom mélange Spiced pumpkin butter and bread
Hard Cheese Cheddar, Comté, Manchego, Parmigiano-Reggiano	Apple slices (local) Dried pineapple	*Red Onion Marmalade Stone ground mustard	Smoked beef jerky Marcona almonds	Guanciale (cured pig jowls) Balsamic vinegar reduction (a syrup)
Blue Cheese Maytag Blue, Fourme d' Ambert, Gorgonzola, Cahel Blue	Pears roasted w/ cardamom Dark chocolate	Bacon Praline * Dovè Spicy Nuts	Bresaola (beef salami) Spicy jerk chicken	Dark cherries (dipped in) white chocolate

LEFT: Charcuterie; the craft of smoking, curing, and salting meat has been around forever, but it's experiencing a rebirth in the artisan food movement. Be sure to add a few pieces of prosciutto di Parma, coppa, pancetta, and soppressata to your cheese platter. Even the old beef jerky is new again, look for some made locally.

RIGHT: The author in the test kitchen with Bocelli on the iPod.
PHOTO CREDIT: *Olivia Farnham*

Don't settle for old stereotypes when it come to wine and cheese. Go beyond and explore an Italian Vermentino or your local Marquette. You will find a cheese that pairs beautifully. All the fun is in the research.

⑪

Pairing Cheese with Wine, Beer, and Beyond

A GREAT WINE OR BEER pairing should not merely enhance the flavor of the beverage; it should also improve your perception of the cheese itself. Both the beverage and the cheese are raised to new heights. Finding the right beverage can be challenging, but the process is fun and informative. Everyone has a different idea of what pairs well.

Top Shelf: Wine or beer, which will reign supreme with the king of cream?

There is an ongoing argument about wine and beer and which beverage reigns superior when it comes to pairing with cheese. The throw-down between the two can at times become very heated. My friend DJ, a food scientist and brewer, weighs in on the side of beer and goes toe-to-toe with me in determining if sipping wine or beer is better suited when nibbling cheese.

DJ: While wine may be the assumed complement to cheese due to years of bias perpetuated at posh gatherings and restaurants, more and more people are defending beer as the superior option. In fact, the acidity and tannins of some wines can render resulting cheese pairings outright disastrous, but it is almost impossible to find such antagonism with beer.

The popularity of beer and cheese pairing, at least in the United States, has paralleled the growth of both the craft-brewing industry and the more recent explosion of artisan cheesemaking. Centuries of evolution and artistic intuition and the recent renaissance under way in both

LEFT: PHOTO CREDIT: *Ora Moore*

the artisan cheese and craft beer industries has resulted in the reemergence of a plethora of traditional and once obscure products. Coupled with modern variations and newly crafted styles, we are provided with an almost endless array of alluring flavor combinations. Beer and cheese are star-crossed lovers that destiny has finally reunited.

Jody: While craft beer *is* making a name for itself as a newcomer in not only its own backyard but in the cheese house as well, wine has been hanging around the cheese board a lot longer. The idea of "sipping" beer is difficult to comprehend. Seems like a beer is meant to be chugged . . . or is that an old stereotype from my college days? Craft, artisan, and small-batch are all names now associated with artisan beer production (cheese production as well), so yeah, "I see some affinity happening here."

The bias you refer to about wine showing up at posh gatherings and white-linen-tablecloth restaurants has long since passed. With the explosion of wine production happening not only in the United States but in what wine aficionados refer to as the "new world" (places like New Zealand, Australia, Oregon, and little old Vermont), accessibility to fine wines at reasonable prices preclude anyone from being left out of the fine wine experience. But star-crossed lovers? Not so much . . . what else have you got, DJ?

DJ: Many argue that the harmony of beer and cheese arises from the fact that both products begin as grass and are subsequently processed (by man or animal in the case of cheese) and fermented. Almost every descriptor used to describe cheese can be used for beer and vice versa, including floral, fruity, lactic, nutty, and even barnyard, among others. These flavors can then be mixed and matched in a complex interplay to produce a whole new taste experience.

Jody: While beer may have an edge over wine with the whole grass to cheese and grass to beer comparison, and thus render a complexity of aromatics you may find on the same sensory wheel, it's not all about fermentation. Wine in its purest form is a grape, off a vine, sun-drenched and swollen, ready to be crafted into a distinctive product. Not unlike the quality milk from animals that have grazed on open pasture, in the sun, brimming over with milk that has exceptional flavor components, just waiting to be dispensed and made into cheese. Both are organic in nature and the raw ingredient for production of wine and cheese.

DJ: In addition to the marked similarities in flavor profiles of beer and cheese, one of the most important attributes that sets beer apart from wine is carbonation. Carbonation not only lifts cheese from the palate, allowing for more effective mixing and thus perception of flavor but also aids in the cleansing of the palate.

Jody: Beer does have carbonation, but so do many styles of starter wines like Prosecco, Crémant, and rosé sparkling wine from France's Alsace region. All have the same effect of cleansing the palate of excess fat from cheese with a high moisture content, which tends to coat the mouth.

Wine pairs exceptionally well with cheese because it has texture and structure, something I find less obvious in beer. The texture and body of wine can be especially pleasing with cheese. As wine opens up, it builds and changes, becoming more alive . . . sound at all like the cheeses on your board sitting out for the prescribed warming time before enjoying? What happen when beer opens up? Where does all that carbonation go? As my red wine is warming and blossoming into something quite different then when first opened, your beer is losing its modest chill and vitality. When a wine's texture is considered at a pairing, for example: a mild, creamy Blue cheese like Bleu d'Auvergne brought to room temperature and paired with a ten-year Dow's Old Tawny Port, smooth, creamy, sweet . . . those two are the star-crossed lovers!

DJ: The body and mouthfeel of beer is a major, albeit less discussed, component of its overall character. Some are thin, some smooth and full. Some beers are crisp while some are heavy. Varying carbonation levels also provide a great deal of variety in terms of mouthfeel. Some beers like stouts even use a blend of nitrogen gas to give the beer a full and smooth feel in contrast to the crisp bite of highly carbonated styles.

As some cheese is ripened before release, so are certain beers. For example, higher alcohol beers need time for the alcohol to mellow out for flavors to emerge. Granted, you can't leave an open beer out for too long or you will end up altering its preferred temperature and losing carbonation, but who wants to wait around for your beverage to blossom? I prefer to enjoy on my own time.

So you be the Top Shelf judge on which beverage reigns supreme with the cream . . . cheese.

Even though it comes down to personal taste, certain guidelines have been proven useful by a majority of enthusiasts. Here are some of those basic truths about pairing wine and beer with cheese.

Wine Pairing Guidelines

When selecting wine to pair with your cheeses for entertaining, the rule of thumb is to go for pleasure. Choose one wine that you know well and is very approachable, a varietal that will be a crowd-pleaser. Choose a second wine that is perhaps a bit unknown; select a wine by region or age or from a private reserve. Just as with cheese, you'll want to serve your wine at the optional temperature for its style. In general reds should be served 2–3 degrees cooler then the room temperature, and white wine not as cool as you think. With the exception of Champagne and other sparkling wine, whites should allowed to warm up a bit and thus open up for you to experience the full bouquet.

A single white wine selection for all the cheeses might be: a Sauvignon Blanc (Pouilly-Fumé). It's elegant but also fresh and crisp and pairs well with a wide range of cheeses. For a single red wine selection, try a young pinot noir, which tends to be lighter, and fruitier than many red wines. Generally speaking, it's rich and complex enough to pair with a wide variety of cheeses but won't bog you down, and it isn't particularly tannic. Whatever wine selection you make should both capture your attention and yet not leave you overpowered, making it a great treat to enjoy with cheese.

- Sparkling wine, Prosecco, Cava, and lighter wines, like a Sauvignon Blanc, pair best with a wide range of cheeses, in particular soft cheeses like fresh Chèvre and surface-ripened and bloomy rinds.
- Fruity white wines (not dry), like a Riesling or unoaked Chardonnay, pair well with a wide range of cheeses, like house tommes and nutty Goudas.
- Red wines, Merlot, and Syrah match best with semi-hard and hard cheeses like Cheddar and pecorino. Even bigger reds like a Zinfandel (at 14.5 percent alcohol) are considered cheese-friendly and may offer pleasent contrasts with the washed-rind and Blue cheeses.
- The more pungent the cheese you choose, the more fortified the wine needs to be; big tastes like big tastes. Most of the sweeter wines and ports, like late harvest, dessert wine, ice ciders, and hard ciders, nicely complement a full range of what you might call "dessert" cheeses, like Blues, washed-rinds and some aged cheddars.

Additionally, Champagnes and sparkling wines can help cleanse the palate when pairing cheeses with a high fat profile like triple creams, fresh Chèvre, and aged Comté. Therefore, the spicy zing of a

ABOVE: Eden Ice Cider is made from traditional and heirloom varieties of apples. The cider is concentrated naturally by the winter cold and then ferments to achieve an excellent balance of sweetness and acidity.   PHOTO CREDIT: *Adeline Druart*

LEFT: Craft beer pairing has become very popular recently and for good reason. With marked similarities in the flavor profiles of beer and cheese, it's a win-win tasting. PHOTO CREDIT: *Olivia Farnham*

Gewürztraminer or the peachy zip of a Riesling is ideal for a pairing if you are selecting a wide range of cheeses for tasting.

Beer Pairing Guidelines

The same guidelines followed in pairing wine and cheese apply to pairing beer and cheese. As with all cheese pairings it is best to start light and move progressively through the tasting, increasing to stronger flavors ending with the boldest. In that same vein it is best to pair lighter, more delicate cheeses with lighter, more delicate beers, and vice versa. This will help prevent one participant from overpowering or muting the other.

* Wheat beers and fresh Chèvre. You can't go wrong beginning a tasting with this delicate cheese paired with a light, refreshing wheat beer. The bright and acidic character of Chèvre is augmented by the citric tartness found in many wheat beers, especially those spiced with coriander and orange peel. Bolder, more complex wheat beers can also be used when pairing with aged and ripened goat cheeses.

* Belgian-style ales and surface-ripened cheese. Belgian-style ales, often delicate yet extremely complex, are described as spicy and fruity and can at times be phenolic. Bloomy-rind varieties, such as Brie and Camembert, pair well with paler, lighter Belgian ales (Belgian Pale Ale, Saisons), in which fruity esters provide contrast to the rich, creamy cheese and complement their earthiness. Just remember that the stronger the cheese is, the stronger the beer's flavors and alcohol content need to be. For particularly strong washed-rind cheeses, choose stronger, darker Belgian ales (Belgian Strong Dark Ale, Dubbel, Tripel, etc.).

* Brown ales are great to pair with many aged semi-hard and hard cheeses. One great combination is brown ale with Alpine cheese, where the focus is on accentuating the creamy and nutty characteristics of the cheese. Depending on the cheese and its age, we may also opt for amber lagers or American Amber ales, which offer a nice balance between toasted malt flavors and restrained fruitiness. I prefer aged cheddar and Gouda with stronger-flavored brown ales and reserve lighter versions for younger styles like Colby.

* American stout with a bold and pungent Blue cheese is a classic ending to any cheese pairing. This requires a beer that can stand up to the strength of this cheese. Select a beer with similar characteristics to port (the quintessential pairing), like a traditional English old ale or Barleywine, which are aged for long periods of time to allow high levels of alcohol to mellow out. Imperial stouts are often my go-to option, but other popular choices include Belgian strong dark ales and double/imperial IPAs.

A few additional reminders when enjoying a cheese pairing:

SMELL: Take a moment to smell the aroma of both the wine or beer and then the cheese individually.

TASTE: The wine or beer first and then the cheese and then together. Allow for them to commingle and develop flavor and textures on your palate.

THE FINISH: Wait a few moments at the end of each sampling for that combination to finish, offering a full range of sensory cues that have evolved in your mouth.

SLOW DOWN: Allow for enough time to enjoy all the cheese (before dinner or if it's a second course)

REFRESH: Provide mineral or natural water at room temperature and small wine crackers or plain French baguette slices to help clear the palate of the previous cheese. This allows for an unbiased impression of the next cheese.

FOLLOW THE SEQUENCE: The cheese has been selected and placed in a certain order. This will ensure you don't electrify your palate with meaty, stinky washed-rind cheese before you've enjoyed the lemony nuances of the fresh Chèvre. Take note of your first impressions (usually correct) with all the different cheeses and then go back and enjoy the pairing out of sequence, see what new combination you can discover.

Enjoy!

BELOW: Create the experience you want, with a simple theme and authentic feel. Give it your own unique character and tone.   PHOTO CREDIT: *Ora Moore*

Have fun while creating a tasting for your friends. Here is a sample of "Cheese Notes" a tasting card you can create for your cheese event or dinner party. It's easy to do; just get on the Web and look up the cheeses you want to present to your guests, find a little information about the cheese—correct name and pronunciation, animal milk it's made from, the state or country that produces it, and the age are all fun to know. Maybe add a bit of the history or tradition behind the cheese, then cut and paste into a word document and voilà! Easy cheese notes!

Blue Cheese and More! A Tasting of Local and International French-Style Cheese

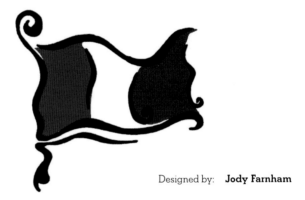

Designed by: **Jody Farnham**

Bonne Bouche Vermont Butter and Cheese Creamery—**Winner Best of Show 2rd Place ACS 2010!** Best goat cheese in the country! This "flagship cheese" of their signature line of goat's milk products is hand-ladled and ash-ripened. It was first introduced in 2001 and has become an American original. It won instant acclaim among cheese lovers, writers, and chefs. Bonne Bouche literally means "good mouthful" and is a French term used to describe a tasty morsel. As this is a young goat cheese, it has a distinct lemony, tangy flavor with a little bite of acidity like a fresh Chèvre would have. As the cheese ages, it becomes soft and smooth on the mouth, with a pungent creamy goodness. Goat *Wine pairing: Helfrich, pinot gris—Alsace, France 2007*

Tarentaise Spring Brook Farm—**Winner Best of Show 3rd Place ACS 2010!** This unique American farmstead cheese reflects the terroir of southern Vermont and the work of John and Janine Putnam at Thistle Hill Farm. The combination of climate, cows, feed, and the traditional unmechanized methods of making Tarentaise results in a cheese that can be most closely associated with the Alpine cheeses of France. This cheese is made from certified organic milk from grass-fed Jersey cows. Raw Cow. *Wine Pairing: JJ Vincent, Bourgogne Blanc 2008 Cotes du Beaune, France*

Tomme de Savoie Fromagerie Edouard Conus—A semifirm cow's-milk cheese made in the valley of the Savoie in the French Alps. It has a delightfully nutty flavor and a citrus tang, a smooth paste that melts in your mouth. The hard, powdery rind has an earthy aroma and is usually speckled with many types of indigenous and beneficial molds. The aroma is strongly grassy, with mushrooms and caramel. Raw cow. *Wine Pairing: JJ Vincent, Bourgogne Blanc 2008 Cotes du Beaune, France*

Comté Marcel Petite-Essex St—An ancient French gourmet cheese, it is made in the Massif of the Jura, a region composed of mountains situated in Franche-Comté, which lies between the Vosges and the Haute-Savoie. The Montbéliard cow is the only breed of cattle whose milk is authorized for making Comté. The cheese is hard, straw-colored, contains some medium-size holes, and has a tendency to crack on cutting. Comté has a floral aroma with nutty flavors developing in the more mature cheese. The taste is full of nuts and toffee with a lovely long and salty finish. Raw Cow *Wine pairing: Mas Des Dames, La Dame 2006—Laguedoc France 2006*

Capri Classic Blue Log Westfield Farm—A small artisan cheese operation in Hubbardston, Massachusetts, founded by Bob Stetson. Unlike most Blue cheeses, Classic Blue doesn't have any blue veins running through its interior. The logs are placed in curing cabinets, with temperature and humidity controls. The blue mold grows almost exclusively on the outside of the cheese. As the logs begin to ripen, the cheese softens form the outside to the inside. Fine grained in texture, it has a rich and tangy flavor, but is still mild for a Blue cheese. This cheese is made with local pasteurized *goat's milk*. Goat ***Wine pairing: Mas Des Dames, La Dame 2006—Laguedoc France 2006***

St. Agur Fromagerie des Chaumes—Is made from pasteurized cow's milk in the village of Monts du Velay. It entices you with its naked butteriness and delicate sharpness. It contains 60 percent buttercream, thus qualifying it also as a double-cream cheese. In other words, every bite is sinful. Mild in flavor and not too salty in comparison to other blues, St. Agur appeals to many palates. Due to its creaminess, it melts and spreads easily. Cow. ***Wine pairing: Eden Ice Cider Company West Charleston, Vermont 2009***
 Follow your passion to the cheese shop!

BELOW: A self-guiding wine and cheese pairing is a unique culinary collaboration. Set one up outside in the garden, by the lake, or at a local vineyard.

PHOTO CREDIT: *Ora Moove*

PHOTO CREDIT *Olivia Farnham*

Rockin' the wedge in
the Northeast Kingdom
of Vermont, Cabot
Clothbound.

(12)
Rockin' the Wedge ... Meet the Rock Stars of the Cheese Industry

ROCKIN' THE WEDGE ... *meet the cheese rock stars!*

There are a number of cheesemaker rock stars across the country who have been participating in good on-farm practices and producing high-quality, award-winning cheeses for years. They provide consistent guidance to our ever-evolving industry and mentor newcomers seeking the dream of becoming skilled cheesemakers. Over the years these rock stars have guided the growth of artisan cheese, have seen its potential, and continue to contribute to its integrity and allure. We can only introduce you to a handful in this chapter, but there are many more stars out there rockin' the wedge and helping to sustain the fast-growing pace of the industry. If you cross paths with any of these cheesemakers or have the opportunity to visit their facilities, you will undoubtedly be impressed by their expertise, humility, and passion for all manner of cheese. This is why we think they Rock the Wedge, and we fondly refer them as our rock stars.

Rock on ...

Mozzarella Company

Owner & cheesemaker: Paula Lambert
Dallas, Texas
E-mail: MozzCoManager@aol.com
Website: www.mozzco.com

Rocking and rolling the world over . . . with cheese

Don't be fooled by this Texan's refined demeanor. Paula Lambert is passionate about making the freshest mozzarella cheese possible in the United States, like the creamy, stringy, fresh rounds she swooned over and ate daily while studying in Italy. Anyone suggesting otherwise better get out of her way!

This cookbook author, lecturer, gourmet cooking teacher, and cheesemaker produces about 20,000 pounds of handmade and mixed cheese a year. Lambert began her entrepreneurial journey as all the best do, with passion. Unable to find the fresh, high-quality mozzarella she craved from her travels in Italy, she set out to create and share this fresh rustic cheese with the rest of America. True to her creative spirit, she returned to Perugia, Italy, where she learned how to make mozzarella and ricotta cheeses by hand from Mauro Brufani, Italy's cheesemaking genius. Returning to her home state of Texas her with firsthand knowledge and passion renewed, she created a strategic plan to accomplish her goals. In 1982 the Mozzarella Company band started rocking and rolling the artisan cheese world and doesn't plan to stop anytime soon.

After a slow start in the early years, the consumer mind-set also shifted in the eighties. Chefs became focused on gourmet cooking with local products, and goat's and cow's milk artisan cheeses were becoming popular and highly sought after. With cheesecloth in hand, Lambert was poised to amaze eager newbies with her fresh handmade mozzarella. She quickly got the attention of the artisan industry, winning American Cheese Society Awards annually since 1985. Her pasteurized cow's milk mozzarella remains the standard by which all others are measured. The award-winning Hoja Santa—a fresh goat cheese wrapped in handpicked organic hoja santa leaves—is a classic example of Lambert's creative flavor profile in her cheeses. Hoja Santa imparts subtle hints of her Southern roots with sassafras and anise.

Incorporating nuances from her travels and her culinary background, along with her Southern roots, this mozzarella matriarch's innovative cheese flavor combinations have taken cheesemaking in a new direction, making her one of our rock stars of the artisan cheese stage. In Mexico she learned to make queso blanco, which she laced with spicy green chiles and epazote, and queso Oaxaca, which she flavored with salt and lime. Greece naturally served up feta perfection, adding to Lambert's growing repertoire. She expanded her product line to include traditional Italian cheeses like ricotta, Crescenza, mascarpone, and Scamorza, infusing them with indigenous Tex-Mex flavors and ingredients and giving them a unique flair. They play a drum solo in the mouth with a little kick of pepper and smoky pecans.

The mozzarella Company was established in 1982, and Lambert's legendary status and the national respect she inspires were recognized in 1998 when she was elected to the James Beard Foundation's Who's Who in Food and Beverage in America. The Mozzarella Company has won numerous American Cheese Society and American Dairy Goat Association awards. We think Paula Rocks the Wedge for showing us the true meaning of Texas terroir and for exemplifying what artisan cheese is all about; small batches made by hand, literally! You can find her products via mail order; at the Mozzarella Company home in Dallas, Texas; and at fine restaurants and gourmet shops throughout the United States.

BELOW: Hoja Santa Goat Cheese.

ABOVE: Paula working her magic with mozzarella.

Fromage Flatbread

When it comes to making flatbread pizza, I take the easy route. This recipe is made with store-bought dough. I would rather be spending time in the garden, foraging for tomatoes, baby onions, fresh greens, and herbs than watching the dough rise. Look for fresh, local mozzarella and goat cheeses for this rustic pizza pie; they are well worth the hunt. *Serves 4*

1 package pizza dough (thaw to room temperature)
3 T extra-virgin olive oil
2 fresh Roma tomatoes (or yours), thinly sliced
4 oz baby spinach/mixed greens
2 small white onions, thinly sliced
6 oz fresh mozzarella cheese, slice in disks, then in half 4 oz soft goat cheese, crumbled
6–8 fresh basil leaves, whole ½ C mixed chopped herbs, chive, parsley, thyme, oregano (or your favorites)
Pinch of coarse salt

Preheat oven to 400°F. Brush pizza pan with olive oil and spread dough out, pushing and pulling to fill pan size. Brush the crust with olive oil and sprinkle a bit of salt over the crust. Top with spinach/mixed greens, tomatoes, and onions, and add mozzarella and goat cheese. Place basil leaves uniformly on flatbread, and drizzle with 1 teaspoon of olive oil. Sprinkle chopped herbs evenly over pie. Bake at 400° for 14 –18 minutes, until brown along edges and cheese is bubbling.

Options: For a meatier version add pepperoni, prosciutto, bacon, or ham.

Try with . . .

Off the Vine: Flatbread is eaten year-round, so the wine you sip along with it may be seasonal in nature. Warmer weather brings an appetite-awakening wine like a pinot gris or dry rosé. When cooler weather sets in, try this flatbread with a Louis Jadot Beaujolais-Villages 2008.

Appetite for Ale: American lager tends to be a bit too sweet for flatbreads; try a Vienna-style lager or Negra Modelo, as they have a malty spiciness and sweetness that works well. Anchor Liberty Ale, a hoppy American pale ale, is an excellent beverage with this unctuous pie!

PHOTO CREDIT: *Olivia Farnham*

Rogue Creamery

Owners & Cheesemakers: David Gremmels and Cary Bryant
Central Point, Oregon
E-mail: info@rouguecreamery.com
Website: www.roguecreamery.com/contact.asp

Rock and Rogue . . .
Making the Blues . . .

Rogue Creamery has a reputation not only for making award-winning cheese, but being community-minded, sustainable, and loving. The owners, Cary and David, are two of the nicest guys you'll ever meet. This duet has brought enormous value to the cheese industry with their gentle approach and energetic leadership. David was president of American Cheese Society from 2009 to 2010, and Cary was founding president of the Raw Milk Cheesemakers' Association. They also helped found the Oregon Cheese Guild and created the annual Oregon Cheese Festival.

Championing the cause to save one of the oldest creameries in the United States, the two former corporate characters bought Rogue Creamery in Central Point, Oregon, from its original owners, the Vella family. The idea was to save a part of the community, maintain an outlet for milk producers, and create jobs. Within a year they had created the famed Rogue River Blue cheese and were on their way to national and international acclaim. Rogue River Blue was selected as Best of Show in 2009 at the American Cheese Society competition from more than 1,200 entries.

Bryant has a background in design, and his entrepreneurial spirit first lead him to produce pop-culture refrigerator magnets. He studied microbiology and chemistry at the University of Washington, more akin to the skill set needed in the creamery these days. David was a high-profile designer as well, working at his dream job for Harry & David; he has been ranked as one of the top ten furniture designers in the country. The duo came together on one subject; they want to produce something original that had nutritious value and did not end up in a landfill somewhere. Voilà, cheese!

These two risk-taking, community-responsive guys are among the rock stars of the Blue and Cheddar cheese milieu in the United States. Under the tutelage of their mentor, Ig Vella, David and Cary, although completely inexperienced in artisan cheesemaking, hit a high note immediately, winning "Best Blue Cheese" at the World Cheese Awards in 2003. Their confidence and spirit speak to the overall movement of artisan cheese in this country. They believed in the possibilities of salvaging the old creamery. With knowledge, guidance, and persistence they made their dream come true.

ABOVE: The happy couple, fresh from harvesting Syrah grape leaves for their Rogue River Blue.

This exemplifies a common belief among the rock stars of the industry, a sense of "yeah, we can do that, now let's roll up our sleeves and get to work."

Rogue specializes in raw and pasteurized cow's-milk Cheddar, but their Blues are their hit parade. They produce Rogue River Blue (aged twelve months), Oregonzola Blue (aged four months), Crater Lake Blue (aged three months), Smoky Blue (aged four months), and Echo Mountain Blue (aged six months). Their products are available on-site and at fine food retailers nationwide.

Rogue Creamery was established in 2001 and Rocks the Wedge everyday by stepping out to the edge to see what can be done next to enhance and move the cheese industry forward. Cary and David take risks, calculated ones, and believe in the heritage and traditions of artisan cheesemaking. They rock because they are innovative and *loving*.

Stuffed Smoky Blue Cheese Burger

These "stuffed" burgers are crammed with smoky Blue cheese and spicy goodness. The cheese is blended directly into the meat for a great dose of tangy Blue cheese flavor in every bite. Rogue Creamery specializes in Blue cheeses—and nobody does it better. Smokey Blue is smoked over hazelnut shells, which impart a smooth and creamy aroma to the meat with just a whiff of smokiness. Burgers are bought to new heights when tossed on the hot grill and cooked to juicy perfection. *Makes 4*

1 pound ground beef (go local)	**½ C minced white onion**
4 oz Smoky Blue cheese (most Blues will work)	**2 T Montreal Steak Seasoning (to taste) or mix your own**
4 large buns split and toasted	**4 slices Cheddar cheese (for topping)**
1 T Red Onion Marmalade (see recipe on page 23)	**4 slices smoked cob bacon, pre-cooked**
8 slices fresh avocado	

Mix burger, onion, and cheese together in a large bowl.

Form into four patties of about 4 oz each. Sprinkle with Montreal Steak Seasoning on both sides.

Grill to the perfect doneness for each guest.

Just before taking burgers off, place bacon and Cheddar on top and let melt (optional).

Place burgers on buns and garnish. Note: Although you might generally choose leaner burger meat for hamburgers, I recommend you use burgers with a bit higher fat content, to prevent ending up with a dried-out burger with Blue cheese flavor.

Try with . . .

Off the Vine: Try a chilled French Beaujolais, a light, fruity red wine, or an oaky Chardonnay for a rich flavorful combination.

Appetite for Ale: Try brown ale or a smoky stout beer with chocolate and hazelnut notes.

Vermont Butter & Cheese Creamery

Owners: Bob Reese & Allison Hooper
Cheesemakers: Allison Hooper & Adeline Druart
Websterville, Vermont
Email: info@vermntcreamery.com
Website: www.vermontcreamery.com

Fiddling with French tradition

The winning duo of Hooper and Reese of Vermont Butter and Cheese Creamery has been making French and American cheese lovers everywhere happy with their award-winning line of products for more than twenty-six years. The winning combination consists of Reese's agricultural-business background and the marketing and business savvy, along with Hooper's talents in groundbreaking cheesemaking techniques and ongoing product development in the categories of

ABOVE: Bob and Allison with a few of the kids!

cultured butters and fresh cheeses. Think thick, rich mascarpone decadence in any dish and tangy fromage blanc. As the company name, Vermont *Butter* and Cheese Creamery, indicates, their butters are among the premier salted and unsalted cultured butters in the country. Reese pounded the pavement in New York City, taking their product to master chefs at the best restaurants in the city and convincing them to have this butter in their kitchens for food preparation and on their white linen–covered tables. Now, not only their butter but also all their dairy products can be found in chic eateries, bistros, and fine-dining spots across the country. VBCC has constantly amazed the culinary community by inspiring famous and not-so-famous chefs to use the products to create some amazing culinary delights. Check out their gorgeous cookbook *In a Cheesemakers Kitchen* and become inspired tonight.

Hooper and Reese both embody the passion, excitement, and fearlessness typical of artisan cheesemakers in Vermont and around the country. They are entrepreneurial in spirit and willing to try new ideas. They share their passion for making great cheese with a collaborative of more than twenty farm families that provide them with the goat's and cow's milk they need for their production. Hooper, at the helm of the artisan cheese movement in Vermont and as the president of the American Cheese Society from 2005 to 2008, has been a voice for and mentor to cheesemakers across the United States. She has been instrumental in the continued growth of the industry by encouraging new cheesemakers to join the movement now changing the landscape of American cheese.

Through their pioneering, we now have access to wonderful French-style cheeses. Bonne Bouche (ash-ripened goat cheese), fresh crottin, Bijou (aged crottin), Coupole, and the classic Chèvre: traditional fresh goat cheese. Their cultured butter with sea salt is amazing, with a fat content of 86 percent.

Vermont Butter and Cheese Creamery was established in 1984. We think they Rock the Wedge for their innovative French-style cheesemaking and aging concepts, and for making "the butter of the gods." VBCC's creations have won more than 100 awards nationally and internationally over the past twenty-five years. Their products are available via nationwide distribution.

Strawberry, Blueberry Mascarpone Tart

There is something so appealing about the ruby redness of strawberries and the deep blue of blueberries together in any sweet dessert! Their flavor is so concentrated when eaten warm, heated by the sunlight, straight off the bushes, that it makes you feel like a kid again, and why not? It's summertime and the livin' is easy. This comfort-food dessert is made with some of the best mascarpone in the world, from Vermont Butter and Cheese Creamery. Serve it up with berries from your local patch—a winning combination. *Serves 8*

PHOTO CREDIT: *Jody Farnham*

FILLING AND GLAZE INGREDIENTS:

I pint strawberries	I pint blueberries
½ C sugar	⅓ C confectioners' sugar
I T grated lemon zest	I T lemon juice
I T orange juice	½ tsp pure vanilla extract
I T balsamic vinegar	12 oz mascarpone, cold

Remove stems, hull, and halve or quarter strawberries, depending on size. Stem blueberries if needed.

In a large bowl, combine strawberries, blueberries, granulated sugar, lemon zest, and orange juice.

Place in refrigerator for at least 30 minutes to macerate.

Meanwhile, in a large bowl, combine the remaining lemon juice, mascarpone, vanilla extract, and confectioners' sugar. Mix thoroughly until silky smooth.

Refrigerate until ready to use.

To make the glaze, strain the macerated berries over a small saucepan.

Add balsamic vinegar and heat over medium-high until liquid is reduced by more than half. It should foam and thicken to syrup with in 6–8 minutes.

Let cool to room temperature.

In a large bowl, combine flours, sugar, and salt. Mix together with a whisk to aerate. Add butter and work with a pastry blender until mixture resembles coarse meal. In a small bowl, beat together egg yolks and 3 tablespoons ice water.

Drizzle liquid mixture into dry ingredients. Mix until dough comes together. If too dry, 1 tablespoon ice water can be added.

TART INGREDIENTS

1 C all-purpose flour	¼ C whole-wheat pastry flour *
3 T granulated sugar	½ C (1 stick) unsalted butter, chilled, cut into small pieces
2 egg yolks	3–4 T ice water
Pinch of salt	

Form the dough into a flat disk and wrap in plastic. Chill for at least 1 hour before rolling. Preheat oven to 350°F. Roll out tart dough between two pieces of plastic wrap to fit a 10-inch fluted tart pan.

Carefully lay dough over pan.

Press dough up into the sides.

Remove excess dough by running rolling pin or knife over pan.

Chill shell for 10 minutes.

Prick the bottom of the pan all over with a fork.

Bake the shell for 25 minutes, or until golden and cooked through.

Let cool completely on a wire rack before filling.

Optional: Line the crust-filled pan with foil and lay in pie weights. Bake for 10 minutes. Then carefully remove pie weights with foil. Continue to bake until golden brown, about 15 minutes. Let cool completely.

Spread chilled mascarpone mixture in tart shell. Arrange berries on top. Brush with glaze. Serve immediately.

* A small portion of whole-wheat pastry flour in the dough makes the tart shell extra crispy. If whole-wheat flour is not at hand, use all-purpose flour.

Try with . . .

Off the Vine: Dessert and late harvest wines or ports may be a bit too much with this fresh, creamy dessert. The last of your red wine from dinner or an off-dry sherry would finish nicely.

Fiscalini Farms & Fiscalini Cheese Co.

· ·

Owner: John Fiscalini
Cheesemaker: Mariano Gonzales
Modesto, California
E-mail: john@fiscalinifarms.com
Website: www.fiscalinifarms.com

Leader of the Bandage Cheddars . . . rockin' the 60-pound disks

It seems inevitable that John Fiscalini would be a dairyman and a truly ethical one at that. Standing firmly behind their farming and cheesemaking practices at Fiscalini, his family has been in the dairy business since the eighteenth century in Switzerland and here in America. He now owns and operates the 160-acre middle-size dairy farm his father bought in 1914, northwest of Modesto, California. It's grown over the years and is now home to 3,000 Holstein cows, providing milk to the giant Nestlé Food Company. It was the first California dairy certified by the California Dairy Quality Assurance Program for environmental responsibility and the first in the country certified by Validus for compliance in animal welfare. Artisan cheesemaking has become the focus of Fiscalini Farmstead for the past ten years. Stewardship of the land, conservation, and high-quality animal care ("happy cows") have always been parts of Fiscalini's mission and are clearly largely responsible for their success in the cheesemaking end of the operation.

Like many dairy owners, Fiscalini struggled to master the delicate balance and economic realities surrounding milk production and market prices. Expanding to cheesemaking as a means of securing long-term stability and growth was the natural choice. In 2004 Fiscalini Farmstead made its first solo appearance on the cheese-market stage. Overcoming previous challenges in their facility and retooling for small cheese production, Fiscalini and Tom Putler's first attempt was a winner. They partnered to create San Joaquin Gold and topped the charts by receiving a gold medal at London's World Cheese Awards in 2004. They spun another gold in 2005 and a silver in 2006.

Now, entering stage left and joining the band of merry Cheddar makers is none other than the fabled Paraguayan cheese expert, Mariano Gonzales, former head of cheese production at Shelburne Farms, in the heart of Vermont cheese country. Mariano came on board with Farmstead, and took the process in new direction with the creation of Bandage Wrapped Cheddar, a 60-pound wheel of pure genius. It is the largest Cheddar format produced in the United States. The sheer size of the cheese influences

ABOVE: Fiscalini cheese stacks

BELOW: Mariano brushing the cheese.

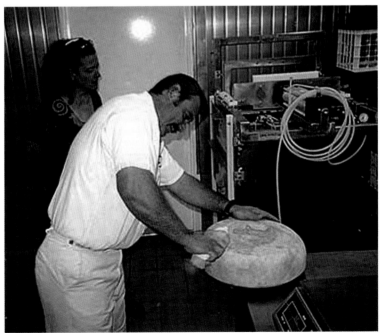

its aging process. Bandage is painstakingly cared for, fine-tuned daily by brushing and turning the truckle for perfect maturity in the aging caves. Bandage Cheddar provides a myriad of cheese profiles, depending on the age at which it is released for sale. The eighteen-month is soft and buttery, with a pale yellow hue; thirty months reveals a full body with notes of smoky caramel and a deep golden interior

Fiscalini Farmstead cheeses include: Bandage Wrapped Cheddar (various ages), San Joaquin Gold (16 months), Lionza (6–7 months), Annunicata (24 months), Fiscalini Cheddar (12 months), and the unique Purple Moon (6 months), which is soaked in Cabernet Sauvignon. Just recently added to the product line are Scamorza smoked mozzarella and plain Bocconcini mozzarella.

We think Fiscalini Farmstead Rocks the Wedge for the quality and care they maintain at their confinement dairy and for the phenomenal partnership John and Mariano have formed between dairyman and cheesemaker. By California standards Fiscalini's is considered a small operation with a big heart. Fiscalini Farmstead Cheeses hold numerous American Cheese Society and World Cheese Awards and are available on-premise, via mail order, and through nationwide distribution.

San Joaquin Gold Cheese-Crusted Biscuits

Pure gold from California! San Joaquin Gold is the perfect cheese choice for baking these golden, delicious biscuits. With a dab of cultured butter, the old-fashioned goodness comes out. You get the feeling you can almost taste the tender grass and smell the sweet fresh air of the exceptional landscape where this cheese is produced. The rush is on. . . *Serves 12*

2 C flour	2 tsp baking powder
½ tsp baking soda	½ tsp salt
½ C unsalted butter, cut into ½-inch cubes	2/3 C buttermilk
½ C pecans, toasted and chopped	1 C shredded San Joaquin Gold cheese (or other creamy, mild Cheddar) divided
1 tsp dried sage	1 tsp fresh thyme leaves (stemmed)
¼ tsp fresh ground pepper	

Heat oven to 425°F; lightly grease a baking sheet.

In a medium bowl, mix together flour, baking soda, baking powder, and salt.

Add butter, cutting into flour mixture with fork and knife or a pastry blender. The mixture should be a coarse meal.

Stir in ½ cup of the shredded cheese, then pour in buttermilk, nuts, herbs, and pepper. Stir until mixture forms a ball, adding a bit more flour if dough is sticky.

Turn out onto a lightly floured board and mold into a 1-inch-thick square.

Sprinkle with remaining ¼ cup of remaining cheese and press it lightly into dough.

Turn dough over and sprinkle the last ¼ cup of cheese over surface.

Cut dough into 10–12 pieces and place on baking sheet.

Bake on center rack for 12 minutes or until light golden brown.

Jasper Hill Farm and The Cellars at Jasper Hill

Owners & Cheesemakers: Mateo and Andy Kehler
Greensboro, Vermont
E-mail: info@jasperhillfarm.com
Website: www.cellarsatjasperhill.com

Rock of Aging . . .

The Kehler brothers spent their childhood summers roaming green hills and splashing the days away at their beloved Caspian Lake summer retreat in the Northeast Kingdom. Over the years as they grew, so did their connection to the land and people of Greensboro, Vermont. Those summer times have turned into a lifetime for them and their young families, having left their homeland of Chile as young teenagers. Jasper Hill Farm has been making award-winning cheese for the past nine years. They rocked the wedge at a young age with the production of stellar cheeses like Bayley Hazen Blue, Cabot Clothbound Cheddar, and Constant Bliss. They have dedicated themselves to a model of on-farm sustainability and local collaboration with other farmers and producers in the area. They reach out to their community, offering opportunities for economic growth and recovery to an area that for many years had been depressed.

The Cellars is a 22,000-square-foot aging facility built into the side of a bedrock mountainside. Conceptually it was born out of a desire to provide small producers in Vermont with a chance for their cheese to become more accessible to the consumer and to compete for their share of the artisan cheese market. For a fair price, the Cellars buys "green cheese" from producers they have worked with; all must comply with standard criteria for access to their caves. The Cellars then takes over the aging, marketing, sales, and distribution of the product . . . all the way to the retail cheese case. This allows the producers to work their farms and make sweet music while making their cheese, which is what they love to do most. The ripening process is often more labor

ABOVE: Andy Kehler checking on the wheels of Clothbound Cheddar in the cellars.   PHOTO CREDIT: *Sara Forest*

intensive than making the cheese itself. The Cellars are set up for the long haul with massive vaults allowing cheese storage in the caves from more than twenty farms. This kind of collaboration remains one of the guiding principles behind Jasper Hill Farm and reflects the Kehlers' commitment to fostering artisan cheesemaking across a wide spectrum of the industry. Their belief is that the more collaborative the venture, the broader the foundation for success in the artisanal cheesemaking industry will be nationwide.

They rock because they have stepped out to the edge of the wedge with their visionary ideas on aging cheese in subterranean cellars and their farm and community mindedness. Their cheese rocks! Try Cabot Clothbound Cheddar (aged 12–18 months), Bayley Hazen Blue (aged 4–6 months), Constant Bliss (aged 2 months), Aspenhurst (aged 4–6 months), Winnimere (aged 2–4 months), and Bartlett Blue (aged 4–6 months).

Jasper Hill Farm was awarded "Best in Show" for its Cabot Clothbound Cheddar in 2006 from the American Cheese Society. The farm's cheeses received first- and second-place ribbons in 2005. Their products are available at fine food retailers nationwide.

Cheddar and Apple Beggar's Purse

When it comes to classic pairings, apples and cheese, Cheddar in particular, is a real win-win. For dessert the palate wants something sweet, but not too sweet, and more savory to finish the meal. Desserts made with simple, fresh ingredients are so appealing. These individual apple delights, called beggar's purses, are sure to please. Serve them on a bed of soft vanilla-bean ice cream or thick creamy mascarpone. *Makes 8.*

6 Honeycrisp (or Granny Smith) apples, about 2 cups cored, peeled, and diced	½ lb butter (room temperature)
3 T white sugar	2 T brown sugar
6 oz grated Cabot Clothbound Cheddar Cheese (or other aged Cheddar)	4 oz pecans, toasted, chopped
4 oz walnuts, toasted, chopped	1 T ground cinnamon
1 tsp vanilla extract	8 5" x 5" puff pastry sheets
¼ C flour (for dusting the pastry board)	Turbinado sugar

Preheat oven to 350°F.

Allow the puff pastry sheets to completely defrost and come to room temperature.

In a medium saucepan melt butter; add sugar, cinnamon, and vanilla, and cook for 4–6 minutes until the butter browns up.

Add nuts and apples, and sauté until apple becomes soft, but not mushy—an additional 5–7 minutes. Stir well to evenly distribute all of the ingredients.

Working on a lightly floured surface, lay out one sheet of dough at a time. Place a generous tablespoon of filling in the middle of the sheet. Sprinkle with handful (2–3 tablespoons) of Cheddar cheese.

Lift the dough and gather on top. Twist a quarter-turn and squeeze slightly to seal.

Tear off excess dough. Cutting is not necessary, as the ragged edges will add to the rustic presentation. For added flair, roll out a thin string of dough and wrap it around the gather at the top of the purse. This will give the illusion of being tied.

Place the purse on a greased cookie sheet. Repeat the process for the remaining pastry sheets. Bake for 10–20 minutes until the crust is puffed and golden brown. Sprinkle with sugar.

Allow to set for 5–7 minutes before serving; insides will be very hot.

Try with . . .

Off the Vine: A beautiful complement to this dessert would be an ice cider; try Eden Ice Cider. Alternatively, try a dry amontillado sherry.

Appetite for Ale: Pyramid's Audacious Apricot Ale is a fruity beer with an amazing apricot fragrance that will bring out the best in the fruit filling. For a coffee flavor companion, try Kona Brewing Company's Pipeline Porter; this one goes beyond a whiff of java to full-blown true coffee taste.

Redwood Hill Farm

· ·

Owner & cheesemaker: Jennifer Lynn Bice
Sebastopol, California
E-mail: contact@redwoodhill.net
Website: www.redwoodhill.com

Goat lady of rock. . . .

Redwood Hill Farm started out as a bottled-fresh milk business in the 60s. Bice's parents built the Sonoma County goat dairy and operated it until 1978, when Jennifer Bice and her husband Steven Schack took ownership of the farm and began pioneering great goat's-milk yogurts and cheeses. In the late eighties Bice established herself quickly by producing a high-quality goat's-milk yogurt, a new product for consumers to try. With interest growing in both yogurt and goat's-milk cheese, it was a big hit. This would become the signature product from the dairy and remains a top-seller and award winner year after year for Redwood Hill Farm & Creamery. Among other winners in her rock star line-up are French-style Chèvres; Bucheret (soft-ripened), Camellia (bloomy-rind), and the delicate California Crottin. She makes feta and a Tomme de Chèvre as well.

Twenty-two years ago, before Bice began to make goat cheese, it was hard to image the tremendous popularity goat cheese has come to enjoy. Goat cheeses were once an exclusively European domain. Bice took up the challenge and has affected the industry with her pioneering ways. She has found the right lifestyle balance on the farm, overcoming the challenges presented by farm life and business life and continuing to be innovative with her cheesemaking. She stands as an impeccable model and mentor for people seeking to become cheesemakers. Her genuine nurturing of and care for the goats she keeps, combined with a refined breeding protocol of

RIGHT: Jennifer Lyn and Jenjambalya.

integrating a variety of breeds, are beyond reproach. She works with Alpine, LaMancha, Nubian, and Saanen dairy goats to ensure the desired and delicate balance of milk quality required for her cheese production. Redwood Hill Farm & Creamery was the first Certified Humane® goat dairy in the United States, certified by third-party certifier Humane Farm Animal Care, considered to be the gold standard. Her passion, hard work, and entrepreneurial spirit have helped to drive the goat cheese category to new heights.

ABOVE: Camellia.

Through her early association with Slow Food USA and more recently Slow Food RAFT (Renewing America's Food Traditions) project, Bice reminds us of the value of the farm-to-table movement. Her overarching philosophy of cheesemaking, farming, and living in harmony with the land has contributed tremendously to the "eat local" mantra and has helped propel the farm-to-fork movement to the culinary acclaim it now enjoys.

Redwood Hill Farm Creamery was established in 1968 as a goat dairy and in 1988 as an artisan cheesemaking stronghold. We think Jennifer Rocks the Wedge for her amazing work ethic, perseverance, and pure love of goats! Redwood Hill holds numerous American cheesemaking awards. Cheese can be purchased by mail order and at local high-end retailers.

Planked Grilled Brie with Tomato Basil Jam

Plank grilling has been around for hundreds of years; usually salmon has ended up on the planks, but not anymore! Bloomy-rind cheeses, like Bries and Camemberts (as they are built to hold the warm, gooey goodness inside while grilling), are being grilled up and served across the country. This recipe is paired perfectly with a family favorite, Pat's Tomato Basil Jam, made of the summer's sweetest tomatoes and lush bushy basil from the garden. Warm, savory, and sweet grilling! *Serves 8*

2 5–6 oz Brie cheese wheels (or try Redwood Hill Farm Camellia)	I pint Pat's Tomato Basil Jam (see recipe, opposite)
6 sprigs of fresh thyme	I–2 fresh baguette breads, sliced
Cedar grilling plank 7" x 7" (maple or cherry will impart those flavors)	

Soak the cedar plank in cold water for a minimum of 1 hour.

Preheat grill to medium heat, about 400°F.

Remove plank from water.

Place wheels of Brie on plank, evenly spaced.

Spoon 3 tablespoons of the jam over the top of each wheel, and place three sprigs of thyme on top of jam on each wheel.

Place plank on grill and close lid. Plank cheese for 10–15 minutes, until cheese is browning and slightly puffy; topping will bubble up a bit.

Remove plank from grill and allow to cool for 1 or 2 minutes.

Serve immediately with fresh sliced baguette, a few spoons, and lots of napkins!

Note: If the plank catches fire around the edges, use a spray bottle of water to put out the flames.

Pat's Tomato Basil Jam

This is a classic late-summer jam from my mom, Pat's, collection. It's nice to put by for the fall and winter months, using up all those tomatoes you couldn't fit into salads and sauces. The lemon zest brightens the earthy goodness of the classic basil and tomato pairing; spooning it on your planked grilled cheese is . . . well, the tops! *Makes 5–6 pints*

3 lbs tomatoes (6–7 large tomatoes), peeled and chopped	2¾ C white sugar
2 Meyer lemons, juice of both, zest of one	2 C basil leaves, washed, stemmed
1 2-oz package pectin	1 tsp salt
6 pint jars, sterilized*	

Wash tomatoes in cool running water. Remove skins by dipping in boiling water for 30–60 seconds or until skins split. Dip in cold water, then slip off skins and remove cores.

Place tomatoes, sugar, lemon juice, lemon zest, and salt in a 6- to 8-quart heavy-bottom saucepot. Add the pectin and stir in. Place over medium-high heat and bring to a full rolling boil (a rolling boil is one you can't stir down), stirring constantly to prevent burning.

Add basil and cook for 8–10 more minutes.

Remove from heat and skim off the foam and fill jars, cap, and cool. This jam can be refrigerated for up to three months.

*Refer to usual practices of jam making and jar preparation.

NOTE: This jam is so delicious you can eat it for breakfast, lunch, and dinner. Try it on toasted bread with crumbled Blue or goat cheese.

Try with . . .

Off the Vine: The baked goodness will bring out the mushroomy notes in this dish, and the unctuous tomato jam will heighten the flavors—a true umami combination. Try a Merlot from the Right Bank of Bordeaux from Bougon or a Da Vinci Chianti, or Chianti Classico from producers such as Ruffino. For an exceptional white pairing, try Chateau Saint Michelle Columbia Valley Chardonnay.

Appetite for Ale: Wow, it doesn't get any better than cool beer and grilled Brie. Try a smooth, nutty English brew like Red Hook IPA or a Sierra Nevada Wheat Sierra (Sierra Nevada Brewing Company, California).

Cowgirl Creamery

Owners & Cheesemakers: Sue Conley and Peg Smith
Point Reyes Station, California
E-mail: info@cowgirlcreamery.com
Website: www.cowgirlcreamery.com

Rockin' the Cheese Frontier

Question: What do you get when you take two resourceful hippies from the seventies, a love for cooking with organically grown food, and support of sustainable food systems and toss them around some of the best restaurant kitchens from coast to coast? Answer: The rock stars at Cowgirl Creamery, Sue Conley and Peggy Smith.

Cowgirl Creamery, inspired by the famed Jean D'Alos, Master *affineur* and mentor, has tamed the organic culinary Wild West with its steadfast focus on organic, local ingredients and drive to make the freshest cheese possible. Sue Conley and Peggy Smith produce pasteurized Holstein and Jersey cow's-milk fresh and soft-ripened cheeses from a renovated barn in Point Reyes Station, California. Launched in 1993 as Tomales Bay Foods, it has become a food lovers' haven for locals and tourists alike. The market and cheesemaking facility on-site sell a wide array of regional organic products, as well as the creamery's award-winning cheeses. These include Red Hawk, a triple-cream, washed-rind, fully flavored cheese that took "Best in Show" from the American Cheese Society in 2003.

Nearby Strauss Family Dairy supplies the creamery with fresh milk from cows grazing on pastures distinctive to this hamlet just north of San Francisco. The milk and cream becomes clabbered cottage cheese, fromage blanc, crème fraîche, and quark. The signature cheese produced

LEFT: Mt. Tam.

at Cowgirl is a soft-ripened, lush round called Mt. Tam. Aged four to five weeks, it's a triple cream with a bloomy rind and a creamy, earthy flavor.

When Conley and Smith began fulfilling their dream of making cheese in 1997, they were fortunate to be on the cusp of the appetite and interest blooming in California for locally produced food, including artisan cheese. Consumers had experienced the California wine country, tasted its fruits, experienced blissful fresh-baked bread at new pâtisseries sprouting up, and enjoyed the innovative menu (or lack of one) at Alice Waters's Chez Panisse. The American palate was poised to embrace all that artisan cheese had to offer. In California and across the United States, there seems to be an insatiable desire for bold, new taste combinations, making artisan cheese an alluring culinary rock star experience. "We got lucky. Right about the time we opened Cowgirl Creamery, people were ready to expand their knowledge and appetite for cheese."

Peg and Sue at Cowgirl are bold and resourceful. They Rock the Wedge because they underscore the natural bounty and local agriculture in Marin County and collaborate with local cheesemakers and dairy farms to create a sustainable model not only of cheesemaking success but also of all ag- endeavors.

Cowgirl's soft-ripened cheeses are available at the on-premise retail shop in Points Reyes Station; retail stores at Ferry Plaza Building, San Francisco, and in Washington, D.C.; via mail order; and through national distribution.

Cowgirl's Grilled Cheese

The key to a great grilled-cheese sandwich is patience. The bread needs to be perfectly crisp and the cheeses melted evenly, so slow is the way to go. The combination of the three cheeses in this sandwich makes for a truly gourmet creation; comfort food but with a little panache.
Makes 2 sandwiches

4 large slices farmhouse white loaf	2 ¹/₈ wedge of Cowgirl Creamery Mt. Tam cheese (2 oz of Brie-style cheese)
4 oz creamy fontina cheese, thinly sliced	½ C finely grated Gruyère cheese (Comtè or Tarentaise would be excellent, too)
2 T butter, melted	

Lay all four slices of bread on cutting board, and brush one side of each slice with melted butter.

Flip the buttered sides of the bread down and spread Mt. Tam smoothly across the surface.

Try with . . .

Off the Vine: Climbing Orange (Australia) Shiraz 2005. This jammy, juicy uncomplicated red wine offers plenty of fresh cherry and plum fruit flavor, and more than holds its own with this cheesy sandwich.

Appetite for Ale: Try a stout beer, which has notes of coffee and chocolate but takes on many other flavors like cooked milk and oatmeal. A perfect companion to this sandwich would be Samuel Smith's Double Chocolate Stout or the famed Guinness from Ireland.

Place the fontina slices on the opposite slice of bread, and carefully mound the grated Gruyère cheese on top of the fontina.

Close the sandwich by placing the Mt. Tam slice of bread on the other.

Heat a large skillet over medium-low heat with 1 tablespoon of butter till warm. Carefully set the sandwiches in the skillet. Cook on one side for 8–10 minutes until the bread is browned and crisp. Flip and cook for another 8–10 minutes until the top is crisp and the cheese is melted completely. You will know it's melted when it starts to ooze out the side of the sandwich—yummy!

Crave Brothers Farmstead Cheese
· ·

Owners: George, Charles, Thomas, and Mark Crave
Waterloo, Wisconsin
Cheesemaker: George Crave
E-Mail: info@cravecheese.com
Website: www.cravecheese.com

Rockin' Wisconsin with Farmstead Cheese

Self (*n*)-sus-stain-ing (*adj.*) rock stars. It's OK if you can't manage that mouthful; it's pronounced "The Crave Brothers Farmstead Cheese." This Wisconsin family dairy began in 1980 when they bought a 300-acre Waterloo facility. The four brothers divide their talents between bookkeeping/feeding, crop production, herd manage-

ment, and cheese factory management. They purchased the dairy to create an agribusiness and soon realized that, due to the uncertainty of organic milk market prices, expanding to a creamery for cheesemaking was essential to their growth and realizing their dream dairy

farm business. "Farmstead" is the perfect descriptor for what the Crave Brothers have going on in Wisconsin. By definition farmstead means: The entire process takes place on the farm, at one location. The milk is from the farm herd, the cheese is made in the cheesemaking facility on the farm, and the cheese is aged to perfection in a special aging room on the farm. The Crave brothers' farm is the very definition of a farmstead operation.

In 2002 the four brothers bought a creamery and became leaders in the U.S. artisan cheesemaking world, with an emphasis on conservation and sustainable farm practices. On the farm and at the dairy, consideration is given to what is best for the environment, the cows, and the consumer. "Happy cows"—950 in all—are milked at the dairy after grazing on open pasture and home-grown corn, alfalfa, and soybeans. They get lots of exercise and rest on plush, recycled bedding produced on the farm. Care for the environment is the linchpin of this family creamery. The Crave brothers have set the standard in artisan cheesemaking for their sustainable practices, including the use of an anaerobic (oxygenfree) manure digester. All of the energy needed to run the farm, cheesemaking facility, and more than 100 surrounding buildings is generated by the manure digester on the farm. This computer-controlled system breaks down organic waste in a process that ultimately produces gas. The gas can then be burned like natural gas, thus generating energy. It a sweet deal, too, as the digester reduces odor from the manure and produces liquid fertilizer for use on the fields and solid by-products like dry organic bedding for the cows. This is a model of farm efficiency coming full circle.

Awarded the great honor of the World Dairy Expo's 2008 Dairymen of the year, these French-Irish brothers harkened back to their roots when they created these European-style washed-rind cheeses. Petit Frere, meaning "little brother" in French, is a smaller version of the soft-ripened big bro Les Freres, aged three to ten weeks. This cheese was inspired by Reblochon and Saint-Nectaire, famed cheeses of France, and by Ireland's Gubbeen cheese, produced by Giana Ferguson of West Cork.

George and his brothers Rock the Wedge with their incredible model of on-farm energy efficiency and conservation and by honoring family farming traditions in the fields and in the cheese house. If you're craving more Crave Brothers cheeses, check out their star-studded product line, which includes classic mascarpone and mozzarella in many sizes—perline (pearl), ciliegine (cherry), and Bocconcici (ball). They also make Farmer's Rope (mozzarella string cheese). Farmstead cheeses are available from the dairy and through limited national distribution.

Macaroni and Cheese, Brie-style

Brie may not come to mind when you think of making creamy, comforting macaroni and cheese. Cheddar comes to mind, or Swiss cheese perhaps? However, in this recipe Brie becomes a super-creamy alternative, especially when paired with earthy mushrooms and the meaty goodness of toasted walnuts. Still sounds pretty comforting! *Serves 6*

I lb package of pasta (use a medium shell to capture the sauce or corkscrew)	2 slices whole-wheat bread, toasted
I T butter	½ C walnuts, toasted and chopped
I 8-oz wheel Petite Frere (or another Brie-style cheese)	I T olive oil
2 garlic cloves, minced	½ lb mushrooms, quartered
¼ C dry white wine	2 T flour
I C milk (whole or 2%)	½ C Gruyère cheese, shredded (Swiss or Parmigiano-Reggiano will work)
Coarse salt and pepper to taste	

Preheat oven to 325°F. In large pot of water, cook the pasta, drain, and set aside. Meanwhile, in a food processor, grind the toast into crumbs, add 1 tablespoon olive oil and nuts, and pulse until chopped fine. With a grater, remove the rind of the Brie, cut the cheese into 1-inch pieces, and set aside.

In a large saucepan, heat olive oil and butter over medium heat. Add the garlic and cook until fragrant, about 2 minutes. Add the mushrooms and pinch of salt. Cook mushrooms for about 5 minutes until they begin to release their juices; add the white wine and cook an additional 3 minutes. Remove from heat, and, using a slotted spoon, remove mushrooms. Place them in a bowl and set aside. Return pan to heat and add the flour and cook for 1 minute over medium heat. Add the milk, whisking the mixture until the flour has dissolved and the liquid begins to thicken, 3–4 minutes. Remove pan from heat, add the Brie cheese pieces, and stir until cheese has melted.

Add the cooked paste to the cheese mixture and stir in reserved mushrooms. Pour the paste mixture into a 9" x 7" baking dish or divide into six individual-serving bowls. Top with breadcrumb mixture. Place in oven and bake for 20 minutes.

Try with . . .

Off the Vine: For a buttery match to this dish, choose a Chardonnay without big oak; on the light side, a New Zealand Sauvignon Blanc would be delightful. For a red, choose one with medium-weight tannins, such as a Merlot from the West Coast.

Appetite for Ale: Try a Belgian lager like Stella Artois, or a hoppy American microbrew IPA such as Victory's Hop Devil. This creamy pasta goes well with a crisp, hard apple or pear cider.

Willow Hill Farm
· ·

Owners: David Phinney and Willow Smart Milton, Vermont
E-mail: info@ sheepcheese.com
Website: www.sheepcheese.com

Rockin' the Green Mountains

Willow Smart, cheesemaking diva of the Green Mountains, is an eighth-generation farmer from Hawaii who decided to settle in Vermont to make sheep's-milk cheeses that rival the ones she had tasted in Italy. Willow and her husband David, a local guy from just down the road, built a stone cheese-aging cave into the side of one of their hills in 1999. Their moss- and vine-covered cheese cave is a natural thing of beauty. The small underground cave provides the optimal humidity and temperature control for the cheeses. It is constructed out of concrete, eight feet underground, with a back wall of Vermont's natural bedrock. There are tiny fissures in the bedrock, where water can seep into the rooms depending on the season aboveground. Although this is a challenge to Willow, the *affineur*, it allows for nuances in each cheese throughout the seasons. They have been aging amazing cheeses like Autumn Oak, one of the first cheeses Willow developed and aged in the cave, ever since.

Willow's Hawaiian background and strong Spanish ties have influenced other cheeses on her hit list! Paniolo, an Abbey-style cheese, was named in honor of the generations of *paniolos*, or Hawaiian cowboys, who have worked on the cheesemaker's 150-year-old family ranch. This aromatic, unctuous cheese is not for the faint of heart. Vaquero Blue, her sheep's- and cow's-milk blend is a cave-ripened Blue cheese that boasts notes of fresh butter and cream with hints of chocolate. Giddyup, girl!

David and Willow are believers in the true roots of the organic movement. They practice meaningful sustainable land management and follow organic practices in their pastures and feed their animals organic

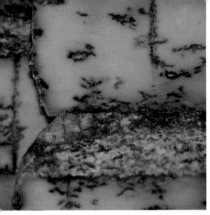

ABOVE: Vaquero Blue.

ABOVE: Summer cheeses by Willow.

grain. They co-op their sheep milk from nearby Bonnieview Farm and supplement their cow's milk with milk from a neighboring dairy as well. Proper care for the animals and the land results in clean milk with wonderful nuances in flavor. This makes beautiful cheese. Their level of commitment to their farm's philosophy is truly inspiring. Regardless of the additional work (and sometimes cost) associated with their sheep and cows, they do things the way they believe they should be done.

In 2006 Willow and David built a new production facility to increase efficiency and production to 15,000 pounds of cheese a year, and there are no breaks between sets at Willow Hill Farm. Besides milking eighty or so sheep and five cows, David also makes a delectable sheep's-milk yogurt, and Willow rocks the fields with her organic blueberry patches. They produce whey-fed pork and Basque-style lamb. They are raised on pasture and harvested earlier than American lamb (which is generally finished off with grain). Grazing diverse pasture grasses contributes to lamb that is delicate, tender, and full of flavor.

Willow and David are rock stars of the industry for rockin' and rollin' on their entire farm, from berries to baby sheep. Willow has been a fantastic role model as a hardworking, passionate cheesemaker for the past fifteen years. Sheep cheese just doesn't get any better than hers . . . even in Italy!

Try some of these products from Willow Hill Farm: sheep's-milk yogurt, Alderbrook, Panialo, Autumn Oak, Blue Moon, Cobble Hill, Fernwood, La Fleurie, Mountain Tomme, Summertomme, Vermont Brebis, and Vaquero Blue (winner of a bronze medal at the 2009 World Cheese Awards).

Stuffed Mushroom with Butternut Cheese

Fresh mushrooms can be a chef's best friends. Whether you need just a little something to dress up a burger, to add to pasta, or to create a whole new dimension of flavor to your sauce, your answer is mushrooms. Mushrooms have a magical appeal to some, and if you are new to the fungi, this recipe may be just the ticket. It's simple and delicious. The cheese we chose has notes of earthy, mushroomy goodness. When baked to a golden brown, these stuffed caps are meaty and satisfying. *Makes 24*

I lb fresh mushrooms with stems, about 24 (stem and set caps aside)	3 T butter, melted
I C bread crumbs	¼ C fresh chopped parsley
I tsp fresh lemon juice	I T canola oil
I garlic clove, crushed	2 oz cream cheese
½ C Butternut cheese, grated (Alpine-style cow's-milk cheese; a mild Swiss will work)	½ C white wine
3 scallions, minced, use white and green part	

Preheat oven to 350°F (175°C). Place caps on baking sheet and set aside. Finely chop mushroom stems.

In a large saucepan, sauté scallions and garlic in oil over medium heat for 3–4 minutes.

Try with . . .

Off the Vine: Try a Cru Beaujolas. Fresh and delicious, the raspberry-mint aroma is a perfect accent to the cheesy baked goodness.
Appetite for Ale: Imperial stouts or Belgian strong ales

Add the butter and let melt, then add the wine and stir to incorporate. Add chopped stems and cook until soft, about 5 minutes.
Reduce heat to low and stir in lemon juice, bread crumbs, parsley, and ¼ cups of Butternut cheese and cream cheese. Combine slowly.
Remove from heat and let cool before working with filling to stuff mushrooms.
Mold a small amount into each cap. Sprinkle each cap with a bit of remaining cheese. Bake uncovered for 20 minutes at 350°F or until the mushrooms are piping hot and liquid starts to form under caps. Serve warm.

Faribault Dairy

Owners: Jeff Jirik, Randy Ochs, Mike Gilbertson
Master cheesemaker: Jeff Jirik
Faribault, Minnesota
Website: www.faribaultdairy.com

Diggin' the Blues . . .

Jeff Jirik strikes me as a true Renaissance man. His easygoing manner and humble character pair well with his incredible knowledge of the science of cheese and the importance of place. He intertwines the art and the science to serenade us with some beautiful blues tones. He's both the successor to a long cheesemaking tradition in Faribault and the co-creator of the contemporary, innovative plant found in Cannon River Valley, Minnesota—once a brewery dug into the side of the sandstone bluffs along the river. Among Minnesota's treasures and the cheese world's natural wonders, the dairy's caves, because of their natural characteristics, are ideal for maturing cheese.

It's not your ordinary sandstone, either. It's pure beach sand deposited there nearly 10,000 years ago. The cave sandstone is unique in that it allows water to migrate through it both horizontally and vertically, adding moisture naturally. The cave walls also have a natural capacity for absorbing ammonia from the air during cheese ripening, allowing for Faribault's clean, piquant flavor profile. These natural attributes are key to ensuring consistent results when aging cheese in the caves.

Jeff says, "Greatness in cheese is consistency, which can only happen with a disciplined attention to details."

This cheese maestro started to create the famed raw cow's-milk Blue cheese at Faribault dairy back in 2001. After making a trial batch with a positive response they looked for a sound relationship with a local co-op for top-quality milk. By 2003, the dairy was launching its now-popular line of Blue cheeses. The plant processes about 180,000 pounds of milk a week, yielding roughly 20,000 pounds of cheese. Faribault continues to look for new opportunities to expand their operation and also to produce specialized batches of cheese . . . one of their current projects in development is a line of organic Blue cheeses made from local organic milk.

Faribault has continued with many of the same practices that made the former plant so successful. They have an in-house lab that does all testing for moisture and salt content. Their exhaustive testing protocol also includes testing every load of milk not only for antibiotics but also for any potentially harmful pathogens. Faribault is the smallest USDA-inspected plant in the country; USDA inspection is an exhaustive process that helps guarantee the product's safety. Faribault feels that, as producers of raw-milk cheese, it is their responsibility to ensure a safe product for their consumers.

We think Jeff Rocks the Wedge because, as he says "We can ride on the edge of the flavor cliff" . . . applause, applause, applause for Jeff and his partners for bringing us a true American terroir Blue cheese. Through their hard work and determination, he and his partners have shown us a world of possibilities for the future of great original American cheeses. Working their way back to the top of the American Blue-cheese charts, they make Amablu (their classic Blue), St. Pete's Select (a more adventurous Blue), and Amablu Gorgonzola. Look for these cheeses in your local stores nationwide.

St. Pete's Blue Cheese Sauce

Any sauce you choose to serve with a rich protein sounds so decadent, but this flavorful sauce made with crumbly Blue cheese is well worth the guilt. You'll get over it . . . especially when you serve this simple, creamy sauce with grilled lamb or beef. *Makes 3 cups*

4 C heavy cream	4 oz crumbly St. Pete's Blue Cheese (not a creamy Blue)
4 T fresh grated Asiago cheese (grated on fine holes)	2 T fresh parsley, chopped
1 T thyme leaves, stemmed	¾ tsp coarse salt
¾ tsp fresh ground pepper	

In a medium saucepan over medium-high heat, bring the heavy cream to a boil. It will not curdle. Continue to boil rapidly for 45–50 minutes, until thick and creamy, occasionally stirring to keep from sticking to bottom of pan.

Remove from the heat and add the cheeses, herbs, and seasonings. Whisk quickly until the cheese is fully melted. Serve over the grilled lamb (see recipe below). This sauce can be kept in the refrigerator for a week or so. When you reheat, warm the sauce over low heat until loose, and then whisk hard to bring the sauce back together.

Grilled Lamb with Kitchen Garden Herbs

This grilled leg of lamb is the main attraction at any meal. No wonder—the rich, full flavor of lamb benefits from the smoky aroma of the grill like no other. Grilling mellows and softens the flavor of lamb and is amazingly easy. This recipe gives specific grilling times so that the lamb is cooked evenly throughout and stays moist and juicy. *Serves 10–12*

8 lb leg of lamb, butterfly-boned (bone removed)	5 gloves of garlic, minced
2 sprigs sage, whole	2 sprigs mint, whole
2 sprigs rosemary, stemmed	3 T olive oil
¾ C stone-ground mustard	2 T orange juice
2 T soy sauce	1 T coarse salt
1 T fresh ground pepper	

In a small-bowl food processor mince garlic, olive oil, mustard, orange juice, soy sauce, salt, and pepper. Place leg of lamb in a heavy ziplock bag (double if you like). Pour the mixture into the bag over the lamb and add the herbs to the bag. Seal tightly and marinate in the fridge for a day or so and up to three days, turning occasionally to coat entire leg.

Preheat grill to medium-high heat for a few minutes, then turn down to medium heat for grilling lamb. Place lamb on grill and close the cover. Cook for 12 minutes on each side. Remove from grill and wrap in heavy-duty aluminum foil. Let the leg rest for 15 minutes; it will continue to cook evenly throughout. The exterior will have a smoky flavor and crispy texture, and the interior of the lamb will be rich with slices ranging from rare to medium-well in doneness.

Try with . . .

Off the Vine: Try a more fruit-driven wine like a younger red Bordeaux, Cabernet/Merlot blend, a Rioja Reserve, or fruitier, lightly oaked Chardonnays, with hints of melon and peach flavors, from France or New Zealand.

Appetite for Ale: A creamy, complex Belgian Trappist ale is outstanding with this buttery dish. They will complement one another. Try Westmalle Tripel.

A Final Irish Blessing

THIRTY YEARS AGO, WHEN the first farmhouse cheeses appeared in West Cork in Ireland we were seen as revivalists. In European terms we had come back to a tradition of small production, regional, raw-milk cheesemaking that for centuries had been signature of European agriculture—ambassadors of regional identy.

In Ireland, since the 1950s dairying had grown out of the cooperative movement into a significant and proud part of Irish agriculture. It transformed our farms into earning and modern homes for our families.

By the 1970s there was a change coming—we wanted Irish food to express our identity, just as our books, our music, and our visual art did. Cheddar and cheap butter were to be challenged by these articulate little cheeses that had so much to say about our country and the people who loved the landscapes that they came from and farmed.

In Ireland, understandably, it came late. Our history had just survived a long colonial past, several famines, and a civil war. These very Irish cheeses came not only as a surprise—as they had such distinctive character—but as welcome evidence of Irish food identity.

Today, across the United States and in Vermont in particular there is something just as exciting happening. Young professionals alongside farmers and dairy experts have identified local food as part of something bigger than a revival. It is at the heart of the future need for foods that will serve us into a new agriculture period and perhaps into the new economies that are now urgently being talked about. My experience has been that you will find qualified instructors who will give you the tools to milk your herds or flocks well, to design and build efficient dairy units, and, of course, to make wonderful cheeses. They will also put you as cheesemakers in a position of real significance in your communities: you will be food makers. They understand the importance of food in the development of a culture, and they understand that cheesemaking is science, but it's a craft as well, and it can be a part of how we express ourselves.

Having skills like cheesemaking can bring farm familes into new and challeging marketplaces. To meet these challenges we need skills—not only the fundamental food safety knowledge of HACCP and good hygeine practices but also the crafting of unique flavors from the land and the animals that graze there. It's a tall order, and you need help to get it right.

In Europe hundreds of years of tradition support this expertise. Ireland and the United States share an historical gap in the evolution of food, so we need to be creative and imaginative, inquisitive and critical. To do this we need good teachers who get what we are doing, and trust the process of education which can bring out our individual talents.

The life of cheesemaking is hard but stimulating work, and the daily process is absolutely facinating. Not one of our colleagues who started making cheese along with our family in the seventies have regretted the decision—in fact we have mostly shared in recent years the best of all harvests—our children have joined us, too!

They have come into the farms as food makers as well. They see a future for their energies and creativity—they love the life of the farmers' markets, the contact with chefs and shop owners, the pride when a prize is won or a customer writes to thank you for the joy your food has brought to their family. They love being part of a solution for the future in our economies and our environments and they quite rightly want to have fun doing it! I do hope you will too.

Giana Ferguson

Gubbeen Farm

Shull, County Cork, Ireland, 2010

BELOW: Gubbeen Cheese Wheels, Gubbeen Farm and Dairy.

Educational Resources

THIS SECTION IS DEDICATED to the new crop of future cheesemakers and dairy farmers: To the youth who will come after us to take up the reins of cheesemaking, farming, and stewardship of the land. There is something remarkable happening in Vermont these days, and my guess is it's true across the country. Young families are bringing new vitality to an old models of family life and farm life. With renewed passion for the land, traditions in farmsteading, raising animals with best practices, and conservation of the land, we see new hope for the old ways. The concept of sustainability is alive and well here in the Green Mountains and around the country. We are swinging back around to the sixties' mind-set in terms of redefining our food sources and the ideals of sustainability—the buzzword of our generation—hoping to ensure that it becomes common language for the next. As parents and educators it's our responsibility and our privilege to share firsthand with the young farmers, cheesemakers, and dairy people what we know well. In teaching them how to milk goats, wean the babies, plant a garden, mend fences, herd sheep, and make cheese, we are modeling how to build relationships with the land, animals, home, and industry that will resonate with our children and their children . . . a priceless gift to the next generations.

Dreaming of becoming a cheesemaker? Here is a coast-to-coast roster of campus classes that can make your dream come true . . .

What do a brain surgeon, an attorney, and an architect all have in common? At least one of each has completed the Basic cheesemaking Certificate Program at the Vermont Institute for Artisan Cheese (VIAC), the nation's first and only comprehensive center devoted exclusively to artisan cheese. At other campus-based cheesemaking courses across the country, you'll find the same enthusiastic group of career-changers from all walks of life. Their differences matter little when it comes to

ABOVE The next generation of Kelher boys. Reed, age six, helps in the barn at Jasper Hill Farm.   PHOTO CREDIT: *Sara Forest*

cheese. Once the hairnets and boots go on, every wannabe cheesemaker is the same—a student of the science and the art of learning to make the best of it. Cheese, that is!

VERMONT

Established in 2004 at the University of Vermont (UVM), the Vermont Institute for Artisan Cheese (VIAC) supports artisan cheese producers and small-farm culture in Vermont and other rural landscapes, nationally and internationally.

To that end, VIAC's cheesemaking Certificate Program consists of five fundamental hands-on courses covering scientific and technical aspects of cheesemaking for beginners, taught by UVM Nutrition and Food Science Department faculty. The courses include Essential Principles and Practices in cheesemaking, which includes Starter Cultures Milk Chemistry (one day), Hygiene and Food Safety in cheesemaking (one day), Cheese Chemistry (two days), and Basic Sensory Evaluation of

Cheeses (one day). (Cost: $2,190, includes tuition for five courses, books, parking, and daily breakfast and lunch.)

"We schedule the courses so participants can complete the certificate within a few months during two sequences of five days and four days each," says Jody Farnham, VIAC's Program Coordinator. "We now offer these basic core courses six times during the year, with enrollment limited to fifteen participants per course."

With an average age of thirty-eight years, VIAC students represent all walks of life, Farnham points out. "Many are baby boomers looking to make career changes, while others embrace the back-to-the-land mindset," she says. "Still others come from fluid-milk-farming families and

BELOW: Herdsman Sam and kids from "We Serve Too!" camp, which offers programming to support families of the deployed military, herd sheep at Shelburne Farms, Vermont. PHOTO CREDIT: *Olivia Farnham*

are looking to add value to their business by learning a sustainable model of converting milk to cheese."

The VIAC Advanced cheesemaking Certificate Program consists of six advanced courses on technical aspects of cheesemaking. They are International Artisan Cheese Practices with international experts (two three-day courses), Advanced Sensory Evaluation (one day), and *affinage* (two days). (Cost: $2,720, includes tuition for six courses, books, parking, and daily breakfast and lunch.)

University of Vermont
Burlington, Vermont
The Vermont Institute for Artisan Cheese
Jody Farnham, Program Coordinator
E-mail: jfarnham@uvm.edu
Phone: (802) 656-8300
www.uvm.edu/viac

NORTH CAROLINA

North Carolina State University (NCSU) hosts the only university-based cheesemaking school in the Southeast, according to Mary Anne Drake, PhD, a professor of sensory analysis and flavor chemistry and dairy foods specialist in the NCSU Department of Food, Bioprocessing and Nutrition Sciences.

The Annual NCSU Hands-on Farmstead cheesemaking Short Course is directed at individuals who are investigating the requirements of farmstead cheesemaking or are prepared to begin or already making farmstead cheese, Drake says.

The Wolfpack program is designed to convey the basic concepts of farmstead cheese production, including basic sanitation and milk processing, basic cheese microbiology, quality control, hands-on cheesemaking, and package-labeling issues.

There's room for twenty students for two days of classroom instruction and one day of cheesemaking in the NCSU Creamery. Along with Drake, instructors in the NCSU offering include David Barbano, PhD, Director of the Northeast Dairy Foods Research Center at Cornell University. (Tuition: $650.00, includes all course materials, plus daily refreshment breaks and lunch. Enrollment limited to twenty students.)

North Carolina State University
Raleigh, North Carolina
Department of Food, Bioprocessing and Nutrition Sciences

Gary Cartwright, Director, Dairy Enterprise System & Pilot Plant Coordinator
   Phone: (919) 513-2488
   Email: gcart@unity.ncsu.edu
   www.ncsu.edu/foodscience

MICHIGAN

Michigan State University (MSU) features an Artisan Hands-on cheesemaking Workshop at the MSU Dairy Plant.

"We plan to establish the cheesemaking workshop as an annual event during spring break on the East Lansing campus," says John Partridge, PhD, Associate Professor and Dairy Food Extension Specialist in the MSU Departments of Food Science and Human Nutrition and Animal Science. Partridge and Bill Robb, MS, MSU Extension senior dairy educator, are the cheesemaking workshop coordinators and lead instructors. Guest instructors are often featured.

The three-day MSU program is designed for people who have never made cheese before and those who want to improve their skills in order to enter the cheese business, Partridge relates. "Participants learn about milk quality, ingredients, processes for making a variety of cheeses, techniques and requirements for aging cheese, and planning to establish a farmstead or artisan cheese business," he says. (Tuition: $425, includes all course materials, plus daily refreshment breaks and lunch.)

Michigan State University
   East Lansing, Michigan
   Department of Food Science & Human Nutrition
   John A. Partridge, PhD, Associate Professor & Dairy Food Extension Specialist
   Phone: (517) 355-7713, extension 179
   E-mail: partridg@msu.edu
   www.fshn.msu.edu

MISSOURI

The Show Me State's University of Missouri hosted its first cheesemaking workshop at the Columbia campus in March 2010. Eighteen people attended the three-day program. (Tuition: $750, included all course materials, plus daily refreshment breaks and lunch.)

"We knocked the dust off our old cheesemaking equipment in the dairy plant and brought in a private consultant to show the students how to make cheese," says Andrew Clarke, PhD, MU associate professor of food science, who organized the workshop. Clarke isn't certain if the Mizzou cheesemaking workshop will become an annual event. "We are discussing the possibility of having another workshop," he says. "But we are just getting our feet wet, and we realize that we need to upgrade our equipment, so we are pursuing our plans one small step at a time."

WISCONSIN

If you want to be a Badger cheesemaker, just come along with me by the bright shining light of the University of Wisconsin (UW). Aptly blending the art and science of cheesemaking, the UW Cheese Technology Short Course, held in Madison in March and October, accommodates fifty-five students per five-day session and includes four days in the classroom and Fridays in the lab. Topics include, among others, milk procurement, plant design, equipment selection, cheesemaking terminology and steps, plus salting, brining, and flavor profiles.

This course is intended for apprentice cheesemakers with at least twelve months' experience or beginning cheesemaking students, including artisan aspirants, with a basic science background, according to John Jaeggi, coordinator of the Cheese Industry and Applications Program at the UW-based Wisconsin Center for Dairy Research (CDR), which facilitates, along with UW Department of Food Science faculty, all the UW dairy industry research and instruction. ($625 Monday–Thursday lectures, $150 optional cheesemaking lab on Friday. Fees include tuition, all course materials, and daily refreshment breaks and lunch.) The lab component, which is not required for the Wisconsin cheesemaker License exam, provides hands-on experience in production of Cheddar, Swiss, mozzarella, Colby, and brick cheeses.

"We are taking high-end cheese science and applying it to cheese plants," says Jaeggi, a third-generation Wisconsin cheesemaker. "Our students are colorful people with a passion for great cheese. Our short courses provide tools, contacts, and knowledge to help them get started in commercial cheesemaking."

"We are constantly revamping the curriculum as updated research results come out of the CDR and Food Science, so the curriculum for that short course is always evolving," says William (Bill) Wendorff, PhD, UW professor emeritus of food science, now serving as a consultant to CDR in administration of the cheese short courses.

Known as America's Dairyland, Wisconsin is the only state that requires a cheesemaker to be licensed to produce cheese in Wisconsin for sale. To qualify for the license, a cheesemaker must have served an eighteen-month apprenticeship under the guidance of a licensed cheesemaker. A student completing the Cheese Technology Short Course gets six month's credit toward this requirement.

"The one other course for artisan cheesemakers would be the Cheese Grading and Evaluation Short Course, which is held in June and November each year," Wendorff adds. "This two-day course covers the principles and practices used in grading natural cheeses." (Tuition: $299, includes all course materials, plus daily refreshment breaks and lunch.)

University of Wisconsin
Madison, Wisconsin
Wisconsin Center for Dairy Research
John Jaeggi, Coordinator, Cheese Industry and Applications Program
Phone: (608) 262-2264
E-mail: jaeggi@cdr.wisc.edu
www.cdr.wisc.edu/shortcourses

Handy to the Twin Cities
Located just 30 miles southeast of the Minneapolis/St. Paul, Minnesota area, the University of Wisconsin-River Falls (UWRF) offers an annual Basic cheesemaking Short Course.

Similar to the UW-Madison Cheese Technology curriculum, the Falcons' hands-on short course is designed for farmstead cheesemakers, as well as apprentice cheesemakers from industry, notes Ranee May, MS, program coordinator for the UWRF Animal and Food Science Department.

Topics covered include milk composition, cheesemaking principles, milk microbiology, pasteurization, regulations, basic analysis, milk and cheese analysis, coagulants, cheese defects, cultures, cleaning and sanitation, and basic labeling requirements. Lab sessions include production of Cheddar cheese, milk and cheese analysis, and sensory evaluation of cheese. Completion of this course provides students six months' credit toward their apprenticeship requirement for the Wisconsin cheesemaker's license. (Tuition: $400, includes all course materials, daily refreshment breaks and lunch, plus one banquet.)

University of Wisconsin–River Falls
River Falls, Wisconsin
Animal and Food Science Department
Ranee May, MS, Program Coordinator
Phone: (715) 425-3704
E-mail: ranee.j.may@uwrf.edu
www.uwrf.edu

UTAH

The Western Dairy Center (WDC) at Utah State University (USU) in Logan, Utah, offers cheesemaking short courses. With the increased interest in artisan cheesemaking, a three-day Artisan cheesemaking Short Course was added in 2003, says Carl Brothersen, MS, associate director of the WDC, founded in 1987.

"As artisan cheesemakers became more sophisticated and knowledgeable, we saw the need to modify the curriculum and offer a basic and advanced course," Brothersen points out. To that end, the WDC is now offering both a Basic cheesemaking Course and an Advanced cheesemaking Course.

The Basic cheesemaking Course is designed for the beginning cheesemaker and those who have never made cheese before, Brothersen says. The basic course includes an introduction to milk, cheese, and dairy cultures, and the steps in cheesemaking. "We spend a day in our pilot plant making cheese the old fashioned way, by hand," Brothersen elaborates. "We limit the course to twelve participants to ensure everyone receives individual attention." (Tuition: $495, includes all course materials, daily lunch, and one dinner.)

The Advanced cheesemaking Course, launched in 2010, is for people who have cheesemaking experience and want to expand their knowledge of milk chemistry, cheese chemistry, curd handling, and correcting manufacturing problems. "We spend two days in our pilot plant making seven different varieties of cheese, representing five different curd handling techniques," Brothersen says. The advanced course is also limited to twelve students. (Tuition: $595, includes course materials, daily lunch and one dinner.)

Utah State University
Logan, Utah
Western Dairy Center

Carl Brothersen, MS, Associate Director
Phone: (435) 797-3466
E-mail: carl.brothersen@usu.edu
www.usu.edu

IDAHO

The University of Idaho (UI) School of Food Science offers an annual two-day Principles of Industrial cheesemaking Workshop for large-scale-plant operators, cheesemakers, quality assurance personnel, and operations personnel. This course is held at the UI Twin Falls Research and Extension Center, Twin Falls, Idaho.

Typically, there is one day of classroom instruction and one day of cheesemaking in a local cheese factory, depending on availability of a suitable cheese factory. Otherwise, the Vandals' workshop consists of two days in the classroom, relates Jeff Kronenberg MS, the UI Extension food processing specialist who oversees and teaches in the Dairy Processing Workshop Series.

Topics include principles of cheesemaking, milk composition, milk coagulants, milk standardization, cheese technology, starter cultures and ingredients, pasteurization, cheese evaluation and defects, yields, and mechanization. (Tuition: $450, includes all course materials and daily refreshment breaks and lunch.)

"Our instructors include nationally recognized experts from academia and industry," Kronenberg says. "In addition to cheesemaking, we offer other dairy-related courses, including pasteurization, dairy HACCP, whey processing, milk drying and evaporation, and Global Food Safety Initiatives standards relative to dairy processing," he points out.

University of Idaho
Moscow, Idaho
School of Food Science
Jeff Kronenberg, MS, Extension Food Processing Specialist, UI Boise
Phone: (208) 364-4937
E-mail: jkron@uidaho.edu
www.techhelp.org or www.cals.uidaho.edu.sfs

WASHINGTON

Washington State University (WSU) hosts its an Annual cheesemaking Shortcourse in Pullman, WA. The Cougars' course best serves established farmstead cheesemakers and advanced large-scale cheese-makers, plus supervisory, management, quality control and marketing personnel from commercial and/or industrial plants, advises Russ Salvadalena, manager of the WSU Creamery.

Focusing on advanced cheesemaking principles, the program promises to touch on filtration technology; cheese yield; the latest flavor discoveries; sanitation; regulatory issues; milk composition; foodborne pathogens; cheese cultures; quality issues; how cheesemaking process steps affect flavor, body, and texture; protecting your product; Cheddar, Italian, Continental, and cottage cheeses; and one full day of hands-on cheesemaking at the WSU Creamery. (Tuition: $750, includes course materials, daily lunch, and one banquet and social hour. Maximum enrollment is twenty-seven students.)

Washington State University
Pullman, Washington
Washington State University Creamery
Russ Salvadalena, Creamery Manager
Phone: (509) 335-7074
E-mail: salvadalena@wsu.edu
www.wsu.edu/creamery/shortcourseinfo.htm

OREGON

Oregon State University (OSU), Corvallis, Oregon, offers beginners Practical Introduction to cheesemaking. The Beavers' course accommodates twenty-five aspiring artisan cheesemakers in OSU's recently renovated pilot plant featuring equipment imported from Holland and France. Launched in 2006, the three-day program covers milk quality, cheesemaking, and troubleshooting, plus regulatory issues involved in setting up a commercial cheese plant, says Lisbeth Goddik, PhD, OSU Extension's dairy-processing specialist.

Day one covers Oregon's dairy industry, milk composition and quality, steps in cheesemaking, introduction to pilot plant equipment, pilot plant cheese production, and cheese anthropology. Day two delves into how to make different cheeses, variations in cheesemaking steps, queso fresco moisture-control production experiment, cheese cultures, pilot plant cheese production, troubleshooting quality problems, and a course evaluation. Day three features regulatory requirements for starting a cheese plant in Oregon, how to work with state regulators, equipment needed, safety considerations, how to clean and sanitize a cheese plant, the cost of starting up a processing plant, cheese tasting and a visit to an artisan cheesemaker. (Tuition: $495, includes all course materials, daily lunch, and snacks.)

Oregon State University
Corvallis, Oregon
Department of Food Science and Technology Dr. Lisbeth Goddik, Extension Dairy Processing Specialist
Phone: (541) 737-8322
E-mail: lisbeth.goddik@oregonstate.edu
www.oregonstate.edu

CALIFORNIA

The Dairy Products Technology Center (DPTC) at California Polytechnic State University (Cal Poly), San Luis Obispo, California, hosts an Annual Dairy Science and Technology Basics for the Farmstead/Artisan cheesemaker Short Course. Held in early September, this landmark offering is available for anyone interested in learning the basic science and technology needed to produce high quality farmstead cheeses, according to Phillip Tong, PhD, a cheesemaking instructor and director of the DPTC, founded in 1986.

"Cal Poly was one of the first universities in the country to offer an artisan farmstead cheesemaking course, beginning in 1999," Tong points out. "Our students include dairy producers, home cheesemakers, cheese buyers and distributors, retired investors who now want to live

"I feel it's really important to study cheese in all its modalities, whether that's through science or experience. Back in 1996, when I started, there was no single place like VIAC to get technical assistance, so what we did was lots of trial and error and feeding reject cheeses to our pigs. Today, cheesemaking is quite different. Beginning cheesemakers are getting up to speed quicker with all the resources now available from books, courses, and the Vermont Institute for Artisan Cheese."—Willow Smart, Willow Hill Farm

off the land, chefs, and food writers, among others. It's always a dynamic group representing many different life experiences."

Geared for small scale production, the four-day program includes an overview of the world of cheese, cheese manufacturing principles, basic chemistry, microbiology and other scientific concepts, milk composition and milk quality, the function of other ingredients in cheese manufacture, equipment, plant layout, and sanitation consid-erations.

Tong says no previous cheesemaking experience is required to enroll in the program, which includes two and a half days in the class-room and one and a half days of hands-on cheesemaking and cheese sampling. Several different cheeses are made each session, such as Cheddar, Monterey Jack, feta, mozzarella, cream cheese, ricotta, and Gouda. "We use these cheeses as a way to highlight different cheesemak-ing principles and techniques," Tong explains. The short course usually

includes a visit to a nearby farmstead cheese operation. (Tuition: $675, includes course materials, daily lunch and snacks, and one wine and cheese reception. Maximum enrollment is thirty-five students.)

California Polytechnic State University
San Luis Obispo, California
Dairy Products Technology Center
Laurie Jacobson, Outreach Specialist
Phone: (805) 305-5056
E-mail: ljacobso@calpoly.edu
www.dptc.calpoly.edu./short.html

"The Big 10" University-Based Cheesemaking Schools at a Glance

California Polytechnic State University
San Luis Obispo, California
Dairy Products Technology Center
Laurie Jacobson, Outreach Specialist
Phone: (805) 305-5056
E-mail: ljacobso@calpoly.edu
www.dptc.calpoly.edu./short.html

University of Idaho
Moscow, Idaho
School of Food Science
Jeff Kronenberg, MS, Extension Food Processing Specialist, UI Boise
Phone: (208) 364-4937
E-mail: jkron@uidaho.edu
www.techhelp.org or www.cals.uidaho.edu.sfs

Michigan State University
East Lansing, Michigan
Department of Food Science and Human Nutrition
John A. Partridge, PhD, Associate Professor & Dairy Food Extension Specialist
Phone: (517) 355-7713, extension 179
E-mail: partridg@msu.edu
www.fshn.msu.edu

North Carolina State University
Raleigh, North Carolina
Department of Food, Bioprocessing and Nutrition Sciences
Gary Cartwright, Director, Dairy Enterprise System & Pilot Plant
Coordinator
Phone: (919) 513-2488
E-mail: gcart@unity.ncsu.edu
www.ncsu.edu/foodscience

Oregon State University
Corvallis, Oregon
Department of Food Science and Technology
Dr. Lisbeth Goddik, Extension Dairy Processing Specialist
Phone: (541) 737-8322
E-mail: lisbeth.goddik@oregonstate.edu
www.oregonstate.edu

Utah State University
Logan, Utah
Western Dairy Center
Carl Brothersen, MS, Associate Director
Phone: (435) 797-3466
E-mail: carl.brothersen@usu.edu
www.usu.edu

University of Vermont
Burlington, Vermont
The Vermont Institute for Artisan Cheese
Jody Farnham, Program Coordinator
Phone: (802) 656-8300
E-mail: jfarnham@uvm.edu
www.uvm.edu/viac

Washington State University
Pullman, Washington
Washington State University Creamery
Russ Salvadalena, Creamery Manager
Phone: (509) 335-7074
E-mail: salvadalena@wsu.edu
www.wsu.edu/creamery/shortcourseinfo.htm

University of Wisconsin
Madison, Wisconsin
Wisconsin Center for Dairy Research
John Jaeggi, Coordinator, Cheese Industry and Applications Program
Phone: (608) 262-2264
E-mail: jaeggi@cdr.wisc.edu
www.cdr.wisc.edu/shortcourses

University of Wisconsin–River Falls
River Falls, Wisconsin
Animal and Food Science Department
Ranee May, MS, Program Coordinator:
Phone: (715) 425-3704
E-mail: ranee.j.may@uwrf.edu
www.uwrf.edu

Compiled by Linda L. Leake, MS, a food safety consultant, auditor, and award-winning freelance journalist based in Wilmington, North Carolina.

BELOW Neil Urie and daughter Tressa, age two, from Bonnieview Farm, making a sale at the farmers' market.

Listing of Guilds, Councils and Associations
California Cheese Guild http://www.cacheeseguild.org/
Maine Cheese Guild http://www.mainecheeseguild.org/
Michigan Cheese Makers Cooperative (Co-op) http://www.
greatlakesgreatcheese.com
New Hampshire Cheesemakers Guild http://www.nhdairypromo.org/
indexNHCheesemakers_2.htm

New York State Farmstead & Artisan cheesemaker's Guild http://www.
    nyfarmcheese.org/
Ontario Cheese Society http://www.ontariocheese.org/
Oregon Cheese Guild http://www.oregoncheeseguild.org/
Pacific North West Cheese Project http://pnwcheese.typepad.com/
Pennsylvania Farmstead and Artisan Cheese Alliance http://www.
    pacheese.org/
Raw Milk Cheesemakers' Association http://www.rawmilkcheese.org/
Societe des Fromage Fins du Quebec http://www.societedesfromages.
    com/
Southern cheesemaker's Guild http://www.southerncheese.com/
Texas cheesemaker Guide (Slow Food Dallas) http://www.
    slowfooddallas.com/sfdTexasCheesePlate.html
Washington Cheese Guild http://www.wacheese.com/
Washington State Cheesemakers http://www.washingtoncheesemakers.
    org/
Wisconsin Specialty Cheese Institute http://www.wisspecialcheese.org/
Vermont Cheese Council http://www.vtcheese.com/

American Cheese Society
2696 South Colorado Boulevard
Suite 570
Denver, CO 80222–5954
Phone: (720) 328-2788
E-mail: info@cheesesociety.org
www.cheesesociety.org

State Dairy Agencies and Marketing Boards
California Dairy Research Foundation
www.cdrf.org

California Milk Advisory Board
www.realcaliforniacheese.com

ILoveCheese.co.uk
www.iLovecheese.co.uk

New England Dairy Promotion Board
www.newenglandcheese.com

Wisconsin Milk Marketing Board
www.wisdairy.com

Other Helpful Resources
American Cheese Society's Social Network: Cheese Wire
http://americancheesesociety.ning.com/

Cheese Forum
www.cheeseforum.org

Sustainable Agriculture Research and Education (SARE)
www.sare.org

LEFT: Dan and Sebastian von Trapp in the cheese room.

RIGHT: The brothers with their award-winning Oma.

The von Trapp Farmstead demonstrates how education can help cheesemaking dreams come true . . .

Sebastian and Daniel von Trapp grew up on the farm, operated by their parents Martin and Kelly, and were concerned about what might happen to it when their parents decided to retire. With the loss of so many dairy farms in Vermont and across the country they were motivated to not only preserve their farm but also to make a go of a farm business in the Waitsfield Valley. The grandsons of Werner and Erika (and great-grandsons of Captain Georg von Trapp—you know, from *The Sound of Music*), today farm 127 acres of land and care for a herd of ninety butterfat-rich Jersey and Ayrshire mixed-breed cows.

Creating a new business opportunity of the family farm led Sebastian back to his college days of studying economics. He reasoned that if they could produced the raw material, in this case milk, turn it into a finished product—say cheese, yogurt, or butter—and align it with a recognizable brand (The Cellars at Jasper Hill), the economics of their dairy farming would change. With a growing demand for Vermont craft-produced foods, cheese in particular, this seemed like the perfect match. The brothers knew they had a name that enjoyed a favorable association with Vermont; so settling on von Trapp Farmstead for their venture they, "hoped the name would open some doors initially, but we knew that, long-term, our product would be judged on its own merits," Sebastian explains.

Setting out to school their imagination in cheesemaking, Sebastian apprenticed with Andy and Mateo Kehler at Jasper Hill Farm in Greensboro, Vermont. Dan was tasked with the challenge to create a plan for rebuilding the farm's milk house and erected a 36-by-24-foot cheese house, attaching both to the existing dairy barn. "Probably the only post-and-beam cheese house in the state," says Dan with a grin. The brothers also traveled to England, where they visited artisan cheesemaking operations throughout the country, took notes, and networked with several of the country's best artisan cheesemakers.

The accumulation of their continued education, traveling, and best farm practices and of course all the cheese sampling has resulted in a wonderful cheese called Oma. Named for their beloved German grandmother, who started the family farm more than 50 years ago, Oma is a raw cow's-milk, washed-rind cheese, with a soft, silky texture that delivers flavor as well. The earthy, buttery paste of this raw-milk cheese

June Guyton, two years old, current cheese lover and future cheesemaker, at Pure Luck Farm.

makes for a beautifully complex flavor profile, not often found in American washed-rind cheeses. Not bad for a first try! The bros are developing a new cheese call Scag Mountain, a raw-milk, natural-rind tomme-style cheese . . . just imagine!

The final piece to the farm business, the cheesemaking operation, comes through their collaboration with The Cellars at Jasper Hill. Oma is aged for a few weeks at the von Trapp Farmstead, then the wheels go to the Cellars to mature in caves built especially for that purpose. There Oma ages for sixty days, during which time the cheese receives the regular brine-washing this style of cheese requires. Then, through a co-branding agreement, the Kehler brothers market and distribute the von Trapps' cheese to cheese shops throughout the United States.

This lovely French cheese, Époisses (ay-PWAHSS) is a washed-rind cheese; you slice the top open and spoon out its unctuous creamy goodness.

Glossary

Acidification: A principal step in the cheesemaking process, in which lactic acid is produced as a by-product of lactic acid bacteria as they break down milk sugars. How cheese is acidified during cheese-making determines the style and quality of the cheese.

Acidity: The intensity of the acid quality of cheese. Acidity can be detected by the tongue or measured by pH. The lower the pH, the higher the acidity of the cheese. Cheeses with excessive concentrations of acid are too sour, which is considered a cheese defect, but mild acidity is usually a pleasant characteristic.

Affineur: *Affinage* specialist who cares for cheeses by washing, turning, and brushing them while they are aging, as well as monitoring flavor profile development.

Aftertaste: Flavor sensation perceived after cheese has been swallowed. A nice, balanced aftertaste is one characteristic of great cheese.

Aging: The ripening process cheeses undergo during which they are held in a carefully controlled environment (such as a cheese cave) to allow the development of microorganisms that are the basis of distinct cheese flavors. *Affinage* is the French term for the tradition of maturing and aging cheeses.

Ammoniated: A cheese that gives off the aroma of ammonia or tastes of ammonia, usually as a result of being overripe or mishandled (i.e. temperature fluctuation). Ammonia is a natural by-product of the aging process and is especially common in washed or bloomy-rind cheeses. A hint of ammonia is not objectionable, but strong ammoniation is.

Aroma: The odor, or smell, of cheese, as perceived directly by the nose. Aroma is closely allied with flavor (some aromatic compounds are perceived retro-nasally when the cheese is in the mouth). Note that certain cheeses with strong odors may be mild in flavor, and vice versa. Also, a cheese's rind may have a different odor than its interior. The aroma of a cheese is most noticeable when it is first cut into. "Taste" words, such as fruity, earthy, floral, lactic, and nutty, can also be used to describe aromas.

Artisan or Artisanal: Handmade cheese, produced in small batches using traditional methods. Artisan cheeses are made from all types of milk. The milk may be from one or more farms.

Ash: Food-grade vegetable charcoal that was originally used to control growth of unwanted molds on the surface of cheese. Now, some cheeses are covered in ash or have an ash vein in the middle of the cheese for extra taste and striking presentation.

Astringency/Astringent: Sensory terms associated with a dry, puckering mouthfeel. A small amount of astringency is expected in some wines, especially young red wines, but in cheese, astringency is usually perceived as an unpleasant characteristic.

Bacteria: Single-celled microorganisms, which can range from dangerous and deadly (i.e., *Listeria monocytogenes*) to extremely healthy and beneficial (i.e., *Lactobacillus acidophilus*). Bacteria (the good ones!) play a major role in cheesemaking, inducing acidification, promoting rind growth, and developing complex flavor and texture profiles. However, if cheese is not properly made or stored, harmful bacteria can grow. Always buy your cheese from licensed cheesemakers and vendors, and avoid unrefrigerated cheeses.

Bloomy rind: Soft-ripened cheese with soft white, moldy rinds. Created by adding *Penicillium candidum* to the cheese surface before aging, or by inoculating the milk. Typical examples are Brie and Camembert.

Brine: Salty water solution used to wash or preserve cheese (i.e., feta)

Casein micelles: The most predominant protein (80 percent) in milk and cheese. Milk separates into curds and whey when casein is broken down by rennet.

Cave: Historically, cheese was aged in real caves. In modern times, a cave can also be a specially calibrated, refrigerated space designed to maintain the precise humidity and temperature levels ideal for aging cheese.

Close: A smooth, unblemished cheese devoid of holes or cracks.

Coagulation: The step in cheesemaking when the milk protein, casein, is clotted by the action of coagulant enzymes or by acid production. The type of coagulation (enzymatic or acid) has a strong effect on the final characteristics of the cheese.

Crystals: Crystals of the amino acid tyrosine, a result of the breakdown of casein (the main protein in milk) as the cheese ripens. Certain aged cheeses, such as Gruyère, Parmigiano-Reggiano, and Piave Vecchio, will have them in abundance. Most cheese lovers consider the crunchy texture one of the delights of aged cheeses.

Curd: The solid portion of coagulated milk.

Enzymes: Protein compounds that act as catalysts in chemical reactions. In cheese, enzymes break down protein and fat in the curd during aging. The enzymes present in the cheese originate from the coagulant (i.e., rennet) and the starter cultures added to the milk. The quality of the milk, and whether it is raw or pasteurized, matters, too.

Farmstead: Cheese produced in small batches using traditional methods and the milk of animals raised on the same premises as the cheese-making operation.

Gel resistance: Clean cut of the coagulum.

Grating cheeses: Hard cheeses, such as Parmesan, Romano, and Asiago, that are well-aged, easily grated, and frequently used in cooking. The maximum moisture content allowed for hard-grating cheeses is 34 percent.

Hard: Hard cheeses are relatively low in moisture content with an inelastic texture. The best styles tend to be well-aged and pack an intensely flavorful punch.

Lactose: Natural sugar found in milk.

Mold: 1) A condition created by the growth of various fungi contributing to the individual character of cheese. Mold (and yeasts) can be inoculated into the cheese or can grow naturally. A moldy character in cheese can be clean and attractive, contributing to the complexity of the flavor; or unpleasantly musty and ammoniated. 2) Hoop or container in which cheese is shaped.

Open: Cheese texture which contains openings and holes in the body (i.e., Swiss cheese).

Organic cheese: Cheese is organic if it is made from organic milk. To be certified as organic, animals must be fed only organic feed and have access to pasture, and cannot be exposed to man-made bovine growth hormone (BGH). Antibiotics may be used to treat animals that are ill, but they must then be segregated from the herd for twelve months.

Paste/Pâte: The interior of a piece or wheel of cheese. Everything except the rind.

Pasteurization: Process of heating milk to a particular temperature for a given length of time as a means of killing off potentially harmful bacteria. Pasteurization is required of all cheeses fewer than sixty days old that are produced in, or imported to, the United States.

Penicillium: This surface mold is used to create rinds that develop with an increasingly soft, buttery texture during aging (i.e., bloomy rinds like Brie and Camembert). Other strains of Penicillium (i.e., *P. roquefortii*) are blue-green molds used in Blue cheeses, such as Gorgonzola or Roquefort, and are responsible for the characteristic piquant flavor of these cheeses.

Piquant: A descriptive term for a sharp-tasting cheese.

Propionic bacteria: Propionibacterium is a strain of bacteria and is sometimes used to develop the holes in cheese. This bacterium reacts to lactose, producing propionic and acetic acids. As a by-product of the chemical reactions between the bacterium and lactose, carbon dioxide is released. The carbon dioxide causes the cheese to bubble; the bubbles become holes as the cheese hardens. The propionic acid also helps to shape flavor profile of the cheese.

Protected Designation of Origin (PDO): This distinct trademark, designate regions protected by the European Union, to ensures that only products genuinely originating in that region are allowed into commerce such as, wine and cheese. Appellation d'origine contrôlée (AOC) used in France, the Denominazione di origine controllata (DOC) for Italy have similar standards for these systems, but generally work parallel to one another.

Raw milk: Milk that has not been pasteurized. Raw milk cheeses must be aged for more than sixty days in accordance with FDA regulations.

Rennet: Enzyme used to coagulate milk in order to separate the curds and whey. There are three types of rennet: Traditional rennet refers to a paste derived from the stomach lining of a calf. There are also "vegetarian" rennets of microbial origin, derived from mold and yeast, and vegetable rennets (i.e., from the cardoon plant).

Rind: Protective, external layer of a cheese. Rinds can be naturally or artificially created. Most rinds are edible (except for wax, of course) but feel free to skip them if you prefer.

Semihard: Cheeses in the semi-hard class deliver a wide range of flavor profiles. These are firm cheeses that begin with a bit of chewiness before melting into a rich, creamy texture.

Specialty cheese: A cheese of limited production, with particular attention paid to natural flavor and texture profiles. Specialty cheeses
may be made from all types of milk, including cow, sheep, and/or
goat, and may include flavorings, such as herbs, spices, fruits, and
nuts.

Starters: Starter cultures consist of varying combinations of lactic acid
bacteria, mold spores, and other microorganisms. When added to
milk, a culture helps to ensure quality by introducing beneficial
organisms to the exclusion of harmful or less-tasty ones. Cultures
work by converting lactose to lactic acid during the cheesemaking
process and cause the breakdown of protein and fat during aging.

Tangy: A descriptive term used to denote a cheese's flavor, usually meaning sharp, acidic, and flavorful.

Terroir: Pronounced tur-WAH, from the French derived from the Latin
word for Earth: *terra*. The term is most commonly used to convey the
larger concept "of the land," or how a given product is produced in
a designated geographical area according to specified, traditional
practices and bears the taste of that particular piece of land or micro-
climate.

Triple Crème: Cream-enriched cheese with a minimum fat content of
75 percent. The majority of triple crèmes are bloomy-rind-style
cheeses.

Turophile: A connoisseur or lover of cheese. It comes from the Greek
words for cheese, *tyros*, and dear or beloved, *philos*.

Umami: Fifth primary element of taste. The other four are sweet, sour,
salty, and bitter. Umami is a Japanese word meaning "savory," and
the flavor is sometimes described as "meatiness" or "deliciousness." The compound responsible for umami flavors is an acid called
glutamic acid.

Washed rind: Washed- or smeared-rind cheeses are often called
"stinky," because they are regularly washed with liquid (i.e., brine,
beer, cider, etc.) during the aging process to promote the growth of
B. Linens, an aromatic bacteria.

Whey: Watery part of milk that separates from the coagulated curds
during the first step of the cheesemaking process. It still contains
most of the milk sugar, or lactose, found in milk, as well as a variety
of proteins. Cheeses made from whey, such as ricotta, form a curd
under the influence of acid and heat.

PHOTO CREDIT: *Olivia Farnham*

Acknowledgments

THANK YOU, thank you, thank you, to all those who have collaborated on this project. Like cheesemaking it was a process.

- My editor Ann Treistman, who is an angel to work with.
- Olivia Farnham for her beautiful photos; she captured what our eyes saw, and her images show wisdom beyond her years. Also, Adeline Druart and Louis Polish for their gorgeous photos.
- Dov'è Design LLC for styling the photo shoots and tasting events.

Plenty of work and enjoyment to be found at the Vermont Cheesemakers' Festival, come join us! PHOTO CREDIT: *Adeline Druart*

· · · · acknowledgments · · · ·

- Profiler Suzanne Loring for her inspired contributions and gracious interviews with the cheesemakers and their families.
- Writers Beth Hill for her work in helping us *Rock the Wedge* with the cheese rock star section and Linda Leake, MS, for schooling our imagination and providing us with a wonderful resource guide.
- Chef Pat Myette for her inspiration, recipe testing and revision, and for her love. To Bill for never failing to eat any of the recipes tested and for his unwavering support.
- Dr. Dennis D'Amico for his contribution to the pairing chapter book.
- The VIAC community of students for coming to school their imagination and learn to make cheese.
- To all those educators and writers who have gone before me in teaching cheesemaking—true inspiration!
- Loyal foodies across the country for their pure enjoyment of all manners of cheese.
- Cheesemakers in every state for their constant pride in keeping this industry safe, healthy, and viable.
- Finally, to—my daughters Lily, Olivia, and Madeline. Merci.

Index

Jody Farnham
PHOTO CREDIT: *Olivia Farnham*